My Last

Robert Nash S.J.

Glendale

ISBN 0 907606 13 X

The Glendale Press
18 Sharavogue
Glenageary Road Upper
Dun Laoghaire
Co. Dublin
Ireland

Nihil Obstat: Hilary Lawton, S.J.

Imprimi Potest:
Dermot Ryan
Archbishop of Dublin
24 January, 1983

Cover by Q Design
Cover Photo by Dermot Beatty

Print Prep (Ireland) Ltd.
17 Brighton Square,
Rathgar, Dublin 6.

Contents

DEDICATION

To Mary Doolan, Little Way Association, Sacred Heart Home, Cedars Road, London — a tribute to her tireless zeal in working for more than twenty years for the missions.

ACKNOWLEDGEMENTS

I wish to express my deep gratitude to Msgr John Magee who enabled me to have a private audience with Pope John Paul II in the fiftieth year of my priesthood.

I wish also to say a special word of thanks to Miss Margaret Beatty who graciously offered to type my manuscript and executed this most difficult task faultlessly.

1 The Birth of an Idea

The first thing to say about this last book of mine is that it probably would never see the light of day only for the gentle persistence of my friend Don Mullan. We are both members of *Action from Ireland*, a group of men and women who try to make some response to the continued cries of anguish which echo in our minds and hearts from the Third World. Our friendship began here, about two years ago. We do not merely listen. We pray. We do all we can to enlist the practical interest of others. We give what financial help we can.

I told Don that I was thinking of writing one last book and this sparked his interest immediately. What did I propose to write about? About prayer, I told him. There has been a great interest and a renewal in prayer in our day and a very sincere wish on the part of many to deepen their prayer-life. This is surely most encouraging and I felt that perhaps I might have some contribution to offer. We talked it over for a while and then Don came up with another idea. Why not write an autobiography, an account of my eight-two years in this world, and devote a substantial portion of it to prayer?

An autobiography! Produce a whole book which, from cover to cover, would talk about me, and only me? Instinctively I boggled at the suggestion. I quoted for him the forthright advice of St. Francis de Sales.

> Speak little about yourself and I keep repeating this with much earnestness. If you are imperfect, humble yourself in secret before God, but do not speak about it. Do not make a parade of it. It is only pride which prompts you to do anything else. Your motive is, that your hearers may not find you to be as bad as you say. The praises they lavish on you are like hot coals flung on the fire to add to your silly vanity. Speak little about yourself. I repeat it once again.

But, greatly daring, may I venture to suggest that I seem to detect a flaw somewhere in the teaching of one of God's greatest saints? Several names rise up in my mind of many close friends of God who had no hesitation in speaking and writing quite a lot about themselves. In St. Paul's many letters there is scarcely a paragraph which does not contain the capital 'I'. What about the hundreds of pages penned by St. Teresa of Avila, all about herself? What about the enthralling *Story of a Soul*, in which St. Thérèse of Lisieux imitates her Holy Mother in this, giving to the whole world a full account of the intimate secrets which passed between Christ and herself, a story which has captivated and fascinated the minds and hearts of millions?

Before me, on my desk as I write, lies the last book of Archbishop Fulton Sheen, which was preceded by some seventy other bulky volumes. He calls it *Treasure in Clay*. It runs to nearly four hundred pages all about himself and what, through his generous co-operation with God's grace, he was able to accomplish in his work for souls. I would be curious to know what sort of reception he got on his first encounter with his brother-bishop Francis of Sales, when they met in heaven. Would Bishop Francis show a slightly-worried countenance and would he have raised his index finger in warning? Would he have expressed, very discreetly, some anxiety and even disapproval, that Bishop Fulton had written that thrilling story all about himself? Did it not smack, just a little, of pride and self-advertisement? Somehow, I don't think he did.

I would deprecate the charge that my motive in writing my last book is, in any way, to boost my ego. If I thought that was so I would drop the pen at once, tear up what I have written so far, dump the small pieces into my waste-paper basket and forget all about it. All I want to do is to proclaim God's abundant mercies to me during more than sixty years of much peace and contentment in the Society of Jesus.

Another reflection also gives me pause. What might be the reactions of some of my brother-Jesuits? They have borne with my foibles, with admirable patience, for more than sixty years. What are they likely to think and feel about this, my latest freak? Jesuits, by and large, are not in the habit of throwing bouquets at each other. I feel sure that if I asked them, and they were willing, they could produce a formidable list of shortcomings, and glaring faults, which would take some of the shine off the picture as I am actually presenting it.

> *Oh, would some power the giftie gie us*
> *To see ourselves as others see us*
> *It would from many a blunder free us*
> *And foolish motion.*

Before moving on let me say that from my dealings with them in the past, I feel certain that they will judge this effort with tolerance and charity, and, maybe, even say a word of encouragement to the author.

The late Father William Doyle, S.J. wrote the *Life* of a fellow-Jesuit, Father Paul Ginhac. It cost him endless trouble and difficulty, but finally it saw the light of day. Here is an entry from Father Doyle's diary:

> I have a feeling that this book will bring much humiliation to me in some way. I have asked Our Lord to make it a source of suffering and I think He will. Not a single Rector has taken notice of my letter except my brother. One criticised the title sharply, but sent no subscription. Yesterday at recreation I gave the book to my Superior. He looked at the cover for a moment but did not even open it, and then passed it on like a sod of turf. I am sure Our Lord intended that, for this Rector is one of my best friends and the kindest of men.

I derive immense inspiration and encouragement from Our Lady. I can see her standing there amid the cypress trees, on the hillside of Ain Karin, outside the house of her cousin Elizabeth. A woman *clothed with the sun*. She lifts her eyes to heaven, and pours out her exquisite hymn of praise. *Sweet singer of Israel*. What is the subject of her song? She foretells that all generations will call her blessed. Why? Precisely because of all the 'great things' that God has bestowed upon her.

Clearly, there is a wise and a holy egoism. Have I overplayed St. Francis de Sales, I wonder? I feel confident he will not hold it against me if I tell him that all I wish for is an unpretentious corner among those many true friends of God who spoke about themselves.

And yet another question poses itself. Will there be many interested in the proposed book? Will it be a Cinderella, a pink elephant, a museum piece, the meanderings of an old man, an embarrassment to the unhappy publisher, gathering dust and more dust, day by day, on his bookshelves? Will it be bought and read? Will it circulate widely and carry its message? Or will it fail to catch on?

A lot of water has gone under the bridge since I saw the light of day. Someone reminded me of this the other day. 'Do you remember, father, telling me that if a plane was sighted over Dublin, people would rush out of their houses in wonder to see it?' I remember. I can go back also to the wonderful Eucharistic Congress in 1932, the highlight of which was the radio message from Pope Pius XI to the million of us gathered together in the Phoenix Park, in Dublin. It astounded us to reflect that we could hear his actual words as he spoke them, over all that distance! We have come a long way from this and young people may not be interested to hear what one of the survivors of that dim and distant past has to say for himself.

All he asks is a fair hearing.

So I begin on 31st July, 1982, feast of St. Ignatius, Founder of the Society of Jesus, and the fifty-first anniversary of my ordination as a priest. I shall aim to finish by the 8th of December 1982, feast of the Immaculate Conception of Our Lady, hoping that St. Francis de Sales will not turn much in his grave during the interval.

2 Beginnings

My father and mother were married at the close of the century. My mother was in her mid-twenties and my father a few years older. She had had a hard upbringing, cruel indeed. She and her two brothers had lost their parents when they were young children. They were entrusted to the tender mercies of a female relative. In the interests of charity I throw a veil over the unChristian treatment experienced at her hands by three helpless orphans.

My mother and father met for the first time at a dance and party held in the house of a mutual friend. She often told me afterwards that she seemed very soon to have a conviction, an intuition, that God had intended them for each other. She was always a most religious woman, with a faith full of life, which had unction in it, but not unctuousness. As I remember her she was as far from being a plaster-saint as she was from the moon. My father was what one would call a staunch, honest-to-God Catholic. His faith was just as sound as hers, though less demonstrative. In this they complemented each other admirably. They married, and my mother used to recall how they were 'walking on air'. Her heart responded swiftly to love; something that was denied her all her life until then. Father had a good, steady job; promotion was promising and probably near. He brought his wife with him to Southampton, where he worked, and they began life together in a state of high optimism.

The first task was to find a suitable house and my father was commissioned to look for one. Negotiations always opened between him and a householder with the same question. Was the house under discussion near to a Catholic Church? It was essential that it should be. Whatever advantages it might have counted for nothing if this one was missing. 'My wife told me to say this'! No use in further negotiations if this condition was not fulfilled. In due course they got just the house they wanted. My mother had forgotten what human affection was, if indeed she ever knew. She was quite transformed, under the influence of a deep love lavished upon her, by a sterling, noble person, whom a generous God had given to her to be her life-partner. One evening, as she heard the click of his latchkey in the door, she rushed out into the hall, bubbling over with excitement and joy, throwing her arms around his neck, bursting with the news that God had sent them their first child.

Their cup of happiness seemed to be overflowing. But it fell and spilled almost before they had time even to sip it. The little girl arrived safely and no name would be considered except the name of the Mother of God. Their first child was Mary Nash.

The home could never be the same again. But the influence of the new arrival was short-lived. God had given her only on loan. He saw fit to take her back to Himself again, after only four short months. They both stood side by side, dazed and incredulous, my father supporting my mother with his arm around her, both of them with eyes rivetted on the empty cot, a melancholy figure of the emptiness eating into their hearts.

Hope revived with the promise of a second child whom they called Kathleen. Sunlight began to stream in through the windows once more. But it proved to be nothing more than a brief prelude to yet another thick cloud. Kathleen joined her little sister in heaven very soon and there was desolation once more in the Nash household.

Next came, incredibly, the death of my father himself. I can still visualise the scene, as she often described it to me in later years, of my father on his deathbed growing ever weaker and my mother utterly alone, in a strange country, without a single human prop to lean upon. How lonely and desolate she must have been. What was she to do? Where was she to turn? She knelt down and tried to pray. She opened her eyes to see her dying husband, unconscious now, as it would seem, for hours. Then she happened to glance through the window. What was this she saw? A priest, ringing at the door of the house beside her. Thanks be to God! She rushed out. 'Father, will you please come in? My husband is dying and I'm all alone in the house'.

Of course he came. He blessed and anointed and absolved

and prayed and stayed with her till the end, and long after. She never ceased thanking God for bringing that unknown priest to her, so unexpectedly, sending him at the right moment, and for the consoling words he spoke to her. My father used to pray every day to Our Lady, 'that I may die on a feast dedicated to you'. His prayer was answered. Mary came for him on 21 November, 1901, feast of her Presentation in the temple. This other son of Mary makes this same prayer constantly.

After my father had been laid to rest my mother sold off the effects which had made their home like a corner of paradise. This opened the wound in her heart deeper still. Two of her children were dead, her husband was dead and her hopes for the future were shattered. Her third child was due to be born in five months time. It was her way to Calvary, but, as in the case of Christ and His Mother, Calvary was not the end, only the prelude to a resurrection even in this life.

Mrs. Peter Lawless, a life-long friend of my mother, invited her to come over to Cork and stay with her until her child was born. God took one Robert Nash from her and sent her another, who, I hope, may have given some consolation to her for the one lying in far-away Southampton. My mother always maintained that I arrived on 23 April, 1902. In the absence of any distinct recollection of the event, I have always taken her word that this is statement of a fact. I was baptised at the Cathedral soon after my birth. I have often seen the house in Panorama Terrace where I began the life which is now coming to a close.

Six weeks after my birth my mother brought me to Limerick. She and her brother Joe set up a little home there in St. Mary's Parish. The parish might be described as a colony 'on its own' living largely its own life, with its own interests, its own social life and with not much concern about other citizens, dwelling in the more aristocratic sections of the city. My mother's unmarried brother, Joseph Kearney, loved me greatly.

I lived in Limerick for seventeen years, after which I entered the Jesuit Novitiate at Rahan, Tullamore. Life was simple and exceedingly happy. Time is a great healer, and, little by little, my dear mother learned to smile again, and laugh and sing and dance, and take her full share in the homely, simple social life of the parish. She had a gift for making friends and maintaining their friendship. She was blessed with a keen sense of humour; she could tell a funny story well, enjoying the telling as much as her listeners enjoyed hearing it. She was simple, childlike, unaffected, unassuming.

I learned later that round about this period a Mr. Very Eligible moved into the picture. He was an excellent man. He admired her and made an offer of marriage, promising to make her very happy. She thanked him, but answered, gently but firmly, that nobody would ever take the place of Robert Nash in her heart.

The Curé of Ars was once asked how he had attained to such love of God and zeal for souls. 'I owe it largely to my mother', he answered and continued, 'Well do I remember how she would visit each of us in turn every night as we lay in bed, make the sign of the cross over each of us, bless us with holy water, and whisper a little prayer into our ears. This is only one example of the care she took with our religious lives. I owe her much'.

Mrs. Vaughan had thirteen children. Every day, for twenty years, she made an hour of prayer before the Blessed Sacrament, begging the Lord to call each of them to the priesthood or the religious state. Of her eight sons six became priests – among them a cardinal and two bishops. All her five daughters became nuns except one, who entered a convent but had to leave owing to bad health.

I make no secret of the fact that if today I am a priest and a Jesuit, I believe I owe my vocation in large measure to the prayers and example of my mother. It was the great prayer and desire of her heart. But I hasten to add that she was consistently careful not to use undue pressure. I recall a lengthy talk we had during which she suggested many other walks in life which I might try. I can now see the wisdom in this. Her example of living faith I cannot forget. I can still see her, morning after morning, returning from the Redemptorist Church in Limerick, where she had offered two Masses, at 6.00 and 6.30 a.m. Heavy rain or snow, bitter east winds – nothing could hold her back. She died when I was forty-seven. In all that time she missed *daily* Holy Communion twice.

As a small boy I attended St. Mary's Convent School in Limerick. Later, I went to St. Munchin's Day School, and later still to the Redemptorist College, also in Limerick. I could never lay claim to being brilliant at my books, though, in fairness to myself, I don't think I was dull. I was a plodder, a middle-of-the-road man. I passed all my exams creditably but without distinction.

I was never any use at the games dear to the hearts of most boys. I think I can say why. My mother, having lost her husband and two little baby daughters, was fairly terrified lest she might lose me too, the only one left. I think now she was over-protective, fearful lest a breath of wind should blow upon me. Looking back, I see clearly that this was a mistake, but, under the circumstances, at least understandable. I have never felt any gap in my life through lack of interest in sport.

I learned to serve Mass at the Redemptorist Church in Limerick. One morning, as I was taking off my surplice in the sacristy, Father Thomas Murphy stood to talk to me. He asked if I had ever thought of becoming a priest. I answered without hesitation. 'Father, I have never thought of anything else. It is the desire of my life'. 'And why don't you come to us?' And he went on to explain the whys and wherefores.

I could not get home quickly enough to tell my mother. I entered the college as a boarder, with the remote idea that I might one day become a Redemptorist priest. The school existed at that time only for boys who thought they *might* have such a calling. It has since developed and is now a secondary college with much increased numbers.

I was there for four years and whatever smattering of secondary education I got was given to me there. I hasten to add that if it was a 'smattering' the devoted priests who taught me were in no way responsible for my limitations in that regard. No one could live at Mount St. Alphonsus, as it was known then and since, no one could visit it for even a short stay, and fail to be profoundly impressed by the spirit of monastic observance which pervaded the place. From five in the morning until ten at night, every hour was tabulated and regulated by the sound of the bell and the observance was as perfect as human frailty, joined to the grace of God, could make it.

We used to be told, I remember, that Redemptorists should be Dominicans abroad, when giving missions and retreats – and they rarely went out of the monastery for any other purpose – and Carthusians at home. Looking back now it seems to me that there was too much regimentation and not enough opportunity to develop the natural gifts of one's character. I think most modern members of the Order would agree. One was fitted into the mould, and if satisfied to go on living in the mould one was doing fine. Nothing more was expected. There was an unbending rigidity and not much opportunity for personal initiative. I also imagine that too much stress was laid on God as Lord, and Judge, and on us as servants, to the detriment of the attitude which makes us look on Him as a loving Father and ourselves as His loving and well-loved children.

A sentence from a spiritual lecture given to us at the time has strangely remained in my mind ever since. I forget the subject of the lecture, but here is the sentence which I am rash enough to criticise. 'In this matter, dear boys, it is well to know where exactly obligation to God ends and where generosity begins!'

A servant will weigh in the balance every service rendered and keep an accurate account of the amount his master is bound to pay for it. A loving son's only concern is to do whatever he thinks will please his father. He dispenses with weights and measures and with account books. A servant asks what he *must* do; a loving son wants only to know what he *can* do; a whole world of difference lies between these two. The servant measures his services by the standards of reason and common sense. The loving son does not deny these or contradict them but his motive transcends them. For the mere servant the Lord is a kind of Shylock; for the son, He is the most lovable of fathers, to serve whom is to reign.

This brings to my mind a pertinent sentence from Thomas à Kempis: *If you rely more upon your own reason than upon the virtue which subjects to Jesus Christ, you will hardly, or not at all, become a spiritual man. For God will have us wholly subject to Him, and to transcend all reasoning by an inflamed love.*

God is not a Shylock.

3 At the Jesuit Halldoor

My story has now reached a stage which I frequently recall and never without a sense of wonderment and deep gratitude to God. I had left the Redemptorist College, but by no means had I given up the idea of becoming a priest. I sought guidance from several sources, especially from an Augustinian, a Father Hennessy, a very good friend of my mother. But there seemed to be no results and the summer was running out. I wanted to have my problem solved so as to be ready to make a fresh start when the colleges would re-open.

One night my mother and I were kneeling together in prayer in the Church of the Jesuit Fathers, in Limerick. She bent over to me and whispered: 'Would you think of trying to become a Jesuit?' My answer was immediate and spontaneous: 'Not at all, mother. One would need a lot of money to pay one's way through the long years of training. As well as that, they accept only the most brilliant scholars'. We resumed our prayers. But I interrupted again. Something seemed to click. 'Maybe, mother, it might be no harm to try, as we are here on the spot, and see what they have to say for themselves.'

So I went around to the hall door and asked if I might see the Father Rector – I did not know his name. He was Father Laurence Potter and to this day I recall with deep gratitude the gracious reception he gave me. I told him my tale, each phase just as it had happened. I stressed the point that I wanted to be a priest at all costs, and I had come to him in the hope that he might be able and willing to help me. Would it be too daring to suggest that the Jesuits might give me a chance?

I realised from the start that I had an attentive, understanding and sympathetic listener. He asked me some questions, about how I had fared in my exams, why precisely did I want to be a priest, what would my mother be able to pay for my years of training, in case the Jesuits accepted me? No use in beating about the bush. As to exams, I had 'got my Leaving' but only just. Why did I want to be a priest? Simply because I loved God very much and wanted to serve and love Him alone. Finally, I said I feared my mother could pay nothing worth talking about. His answer is burned in my memory. 'Your first two answers are fine and the question of fees does not raise an insuperable obstacle'. This is the exact phrase he used. I have remembered it word for word for more than sixty years.

Father Potter went on: 'It seems to me that we shall be delighted to have you and that you ought to be very happy with us. I'll write to our Father Provincial about you and recommend you strongly. I foresee no difficulty. I'll let you know when I hear from him'. That was that. Remember that this good priest had never set eyes upon me before. He knew nothing about me except what I had just told him. I have always felt that the Holy Spirit must have guided him in what to say and what to do on that night. If this was so it meant that God was offering me a vocation as a priest in the Society of Jesus. It was an overpowering thought. It remains the same still, right up to this present moment. Lest I forget, let me say that the two objections I had made to my mother's suggestion fell to the ground. It was not true then and it is not true today, that the Jesuits look for a lot of money before they agree to admit a novice. And secondly, after more than sixty years in the Society, I am no longer deluded by the statement that only brilliant men need apply!

I gave a retreat in that church in Limerick recently and I told my congregation what I am now writing down. I added that I was fairly sure of the actual spot where my mother and I had prayed together on that evening. I had knelt there again during the retreat, I said, to thank God and Our Lady, whom we Jesuits know as Queen and Mother of the Society of Jesus. I thanked them for all they had done, in me and through me, then and ever since.

Soon after my interview with Father Potter, the Provincial, Father Nolan, wrote to him to say that I was to be examined by four Jesuit priests. Their reports were satisfactory. I was accepted. Thus did it come about that on 1 September 1919, I said goodbye to my mother and to my uncle and boarded the evening train from Limerick to Tullamore. On the same train and travelling to the same station and for the same purpose, I met a young man a little older than myself, Harold Craig. He, too, was ordained in due course and has done much excellent work over fifty years as a Jesuit priest. Actually, for the past few years he has been back at square one, at Rahan, or, as Jesuits usually call it, at Tullabeg. He has charge of the public church there, and, to my great joy, I hear much praise of the devotedness with which he serves his people.

He invited me down for his jubilee a little over a year ago. When we stepped into the hall he asked me: 'Do you remember it?' 'Perfectly,' I told him. The scene was as vivid that day as it was then all those years ago. Father Byrne stood there welcoming us. Father Casey there, and Father White over there. I summoned them, all three, from their graves and set them in their places and experienced no difficulty at all in moving back the hands of the clock fifty years.

Until that day I had never before met with any priest who inspired me as did Father George Byrne, our Master of Novices. The Novitiate would last for two full years. At first I was giddy and immature, and, while from the start I admired and respected him deeply, it took some time for the effect of his words and example to sink in. It was not until the Thirty Day Retreat, starting a month after our arrival, that the seed began to take root.

Unquestionably Father Byrne was a man of very deep faith. When he gave us spiritual lectures, or private direction in his room, he was eloquent and fluent, but, above all, there was a ring of conviction in the tone of his voice which could be explained only by the fact that he asked us to do nothing which he did not do himself. Like Christ Our Lord, this priest 'began to *do* and to *teach*'. Years later, when he was an old man, as I am now, I used to tell him: 'If I have any love for Christ and His Mother, any zeal for souls, any high ideals in the spiritual way, I owe all of it to you and to my mother'.

He appreciated this, for there were some splendid Jesuits who did not go along the whole way with him in the spiritual training he was giving us. Readers will understand, I suppose, that the period of novitiate, in every Religious Order, is given over exclusively to the spiritual direction and formation of the novices. For Jesuits, this means a serious consistent effort to grasp the teaching contained in the book of *Spiritual Exercises* as given to them by St. Ignatius. Every novice, a month or so after entering, is presented with a copy of this book. For thirty consecutive days, under the guidance of his Novice Master, he contemplates, in silence and prayer, face to face with God, what that book contains, applying it to his own case. Popes and saints, down through the centuries, have paid high tribute to the principles found in this slender volume, to lift sinners out of their sins, to inspire generous souls with the longing and the determination to become saints.

I could never admit, to this day, that Father Byrne departed in any way from traditional Jesuit teaching. He never gave us anything which was not a development and a flowering of what St. Ignatius handed down in his book. Our Novice Master loved that book, had a profound knowledge of the solid spiritual principles it contains. He lived it himself and spared no effort to encourage us to do the same.

There is a deplorable tendency today to isolate religion from life. The rift is to be expected and explained by the general ignorance of the meaning of religion in practice, on the part of many. The teaching of religion in many of our Catholic schools is pathetically inadequate. The raw undergraduate, with a superficial knowledge of his faith, enters a university whose curriculum lacks any real religious orientation. If he is fortunate enough to avoid the pitfalls of cynicism, the barrenness of anti-clericalism, and the tragedy of religious indifference, he emerges ultimately into a community not fully conscious of his problem or geared to deal with his special needs.

How would St. Ignatius tackle the problem presented by this kind of Catholic? It is beyond question that he would move heaven and earth to induce him to do the *Spiritual Exercises*, if possible for an entire month. 'The book', says the late Archbishop Goodier, 'has been written, not that it may be read, but that, at every step, it might be set aside and put into practice. It has been written with the understanding that he who uses it has by his side an interpreter to explain it to him'.

Nothing could ever shake my conviction that Father George Byrne was an ideal interpreter.

He had the gift of tears. Suddenly, in the middle of a lecture, his voice would break. He would try to control himself and if he did not succeed he would leave the chapel and allow us to go on praying on our own. No question about it that he did actually shed tears on occasions like these. For many Jesuits this was intolerable. Some were inclined to suspect that he was just 'putting on an act' in order to impress us youngsters with his sanctity. Others mocked. I listened once to a lengthy account of a scene during a lecture in which Father George broke into tears and his Jesuit audience into fits of unrestrained derisive laughter. All these considered that the practice was unmanly, not the sort of thing to be expected from the sons of 'the soldier-saint of Loyola', a sugary sentimentality, a mere emotionalism which should be well and truly suppressed.

But what, then, is to be said about the fact that 'Jesus wept'? He wept at the grave of His friend Lazarus, and the bystanders muttered: 'See how He loved him'. He sat on the brow of the Mount of Olives overlooking the guilty city of Jerusalem. The sight drew tears from His eyes and wrung from His heart the plaintive cry about the ingratitude of His people. 'Jerusalem, Jerusalem, how often would I have gathered you, as the hen gathers her chickens under her wings, but you would not have Me.'

What surprises one most of all is that people who bring forward this objection seem to ignore or forget the fact that Ignatius himself shed abundant tears and failed in his efforts to restrain them. They often came when he was saying Mass, and, as a result, it took whole hours, literally, to complete the holy sacrifice. Sometimes, indeed, they prevented him from saying Mass at all. And in his *Spiritual Exercises* he counsels his disciples, on at least two occasions, to pray for the gift of tears – tears of repentance for our own sins, and tears of sympathy with Christ 'Who, for my sake, is going to His sacred Passion'.

One day in the novitiate was more or less a replica of the day which preceded it, and tomorrow would scarcely differ from either. This was by deliberate design, an endurance test intended to give us a taste of a solitary life which we might have to face later on. We were told to write to our immediate relatives once a month. Here is a speciman of what one youth produced: 'My dear Mother, Nothing ever happens down here. So, when you have read this letter, please send it back to me and it will do again for next month!' Another novice, anxious to induce a former school-companion to follow him, added as an argument that 'it's a great life here, and the grub is topping!'

At the end of two years in the Novitiate we took the vows of poverty, chastity, and obedience, and we added a promise which had the force of a vow 'to enter the Society of Jesus, forever to live my life therein'. Thus was the final seal stamped on our lives of consecration. After that, I moved into another part of the house, for a year to brush up my classics. It was an unexciting period except for one experience which was to have a very big influence on my subsequent life, and which is still very much with me in my old age. Let me explain.

In those days we young people were commissioned to preach trial sermons in front of the whole community, Brothers, Priests, and Superiors. It gave us a chance to test our wings, its purpose being to serve as a remote preparation for the time in the dim distance when, as priests, we would address real sermons to real audiences.

When it came to my turn to deliver a sermon, I was told to preach on the parable of the sower. 'The sower went forth to sow his seed. . . .' I prepared it very carefully. When, after supper, I rejoined my colleagues, our Superior, Father John Barragry, was kind enough to congratulate me warmly. 'An excellent sermon; most promising.' I thanked him and he went on: 'Now you know you should get that published. Type it out neatly and send it to the censor. I feel sure he will pass it. If he does, mail it to the *Homiletic Monthly* in New York. You'll find they will gladly accept it and publish it and send you a nice little cheque'.

I went to his room afterwards to ask if he was really serious. 'Of course I am serious. Go right ahead'. Everything worked out exactly as he had promised. In due course I had a reply back from the editor of the *Homiletic Monthly*, in which I was addressed for the first time in my life, as 'Dear Reverend Father' – and me only just getting used to the feeling of the Roman collar! They thanked me for my article. They would willingly publish it. And they had much pleasure in enclosing herewith their usual fee – ten dollars, fifty cents.

Not more pleasure than I had in accepting it! I read that article in print about six times!

That was how I embarked on the apostolate of the pen and readers of this book will not need to be told that I am now on the point of laying the pen down. Much has happened in-between. After the first article I wrote a series of articles for religious magazines like the *Sacred Heart Messenger*, *St. Anthony's Annals* and *The Madonna*. Gradually I moved on to writing pamphlets, and finally, I wrote my first full-length book. Now I am writing my last.

That first full-length book has been followed by many others. They have circulated widely, starting with a thousand or two thousand copies and reaching up to sixty and seventy thousand. The best-selling book among them was *Is Life Worthwhile?* which exceeded 100,000 copies.

I feel horribly afraid lest all this may sound bombastic but I have, I think, sound reasons for taking the risk. One desire I have is to encourage young writers, who should be able to put Christ's message across in the modern language to which I am largely a stranger. The experiences I have had are proof positive that the apostolate of the pen offers a wide potential to reach souls all over the world. The enemies of God realise this and they exploit this area with a zeal and efficiency which must make us feel rather ashamed of our apathy. In saying this I have in mind especially my brother-priests. Why miss this opportunity? Why do we not write more? Over the years I wrote several 'Prie-dieu' books – the Priest at his Prie-dieu; the Nun at her Prie-dieu; the Seminarian at his prie-dieu; everyman at his Prie-dieu. Once, when I was going to Rome, my brethren gave out that the purpose of my visit was to collect material for another – The Pope at his Prie-dieu! It wasn't true, of course! I haven't got around to that one yet!

It is more than thirty years now since Father Thomas Byrne, then our Provincial, suggested that I should write a weekly article for *The Sunday Press*. I have never missed one Sunday in all that time, and the series is now in its thirty-second year and is blooming still! At one stage I told Father McGarry, then Provincial, that I reckoned I had written to date half a million words in *The Sunday Press* and did he not think it was time for me to retire? 'Wait till you've done another half million.' I've done that now. So?

All this gives me immense consolation and fills me with gratitude to God who would seem to have blessed my feeble efforts generously. The apostolate of the pen has opened a world for me, the existence of which I would not have suspected without it. It has paved the way to very many friendships which I greatly prize. Most important and most consoling of all is that I have been repeatedly assured that it has helped souls, stimulating the generous to greater generosity, encouraging apostolic effort, and, crowning all else, acting as a bridge back to God for many a poor soul separated from Him by years of sin.

Let me give, in tabloid form, some typical examples, chosen from a great number. Writing about confession, I stressed the truth that there is no sin which Christ is not willing and eager to forgive, if the sinner will only avail of the marvellous graces contained in this sacrament. I added something like this: 'If you have a difficult confession to make, if you have been a long time away, if you are feeling nervous, then, before you begin, tell the priest just exactly how you feel. If you wish, tell him you read about this way of approach in the *Press* and were assured that the priest would understand how hard it was for you. Here is one reaction which these simple words evoked: 'Dear Father, may the good Lord reward you for that wonderful phone call article in the *Evening Press*. It was written for me. I took your advice. The priest could not have been kinder. I felt as if I was speaking to Christ Himself. He lifted a great weight off my soul'.

Another equally consoling letter reached me more recently. My only regret is that it is unsigned. It speaks for itself. 'Dear Father Nash, I feel compelled to tell you what your writings have done for me. My life was lived far away from God for many many years. The only contact I had with anything spiritual was your 'Phone Call'. For a good while I used to just glance at it with indifference and then pass on to other items, without giving it any serious reflection. However, when through unhappiness and bad luck I was forced to rethink my life, I found that your articles re-instructed me and gave me hope in the love and mercy of God. Every day I ask Jesus in the Blessed Sacrament to give you joy and comfort. I thank you for what you have done for me. Kindly remember me in your prayers . . .'.

I once received a most friendly letter from four young Irishmen working in England. They wrote generously about some things they had read – articles from the *Sunday Press* etc. 'Of course we acknowledge that these are the most important of all. But we think we would like you sometimes to talk about our life in this present world'.

To this I replied: (1) My life as a priest was dedicated to using whatever God may have given me as a guide and inspiration to His love and praise. This must ever be my primary concern. (2) It of course did not imply that I rated the world and its problems as of little importance. There will always be plenty of people to write and speak on these matters, whereas those who focus their attention exclusively on the things of God will always be in a minority.

After three years in Milltown Park each one in our group was assigned to a Jesuit College to train and to teach. My name on the list indicated that my next port of call was to be Australia, which was then a mission of the Irish Province. I was thrilled. I looked forward eagerly to the experience of a new life and a very different country.

There was, of course, the wrench to my mother, and, indeed, to myself. Father McWilliams, then an elderly Jesuit priest in Limerick and greatly respected, declared openly that this assignment was cruel as there were others who could go and not cause this pain. Was he right in this case? I'm not so sure. The hour struck and I took the boat from Dun Laoghaire to London and from London to Melbourne, a trip lasting in those days some four or five weeks.

My mother indeed was to suffer from the very first. I promised, of course, to write to her a number of times before finally setting off. I did so. I knew she intended spending a week or two at the Cistercian Monastery in Roscrea. I addressed each letter accordingly. What she actually had planned to do was to spend about a week in Dublin, and *then* move on to Roscrea. Day after day passed, and no letter! Whatever could have happened? She grew anxious and alarmed. She went to the post office. No letter. In her distress she went to Father Doyle, here in Gardiner Street. He tried to convince her that had there been any kind of accident it would have been reported in the papers. No use. Not logical. Not common sense. But love is like that. . . . Finally, with a heavy heart she took the train for Roscrea. The Brother Porter welcomed her, adding casually: 'Mrs. Nash, we have two or three letters waiting for you here in the office'.

The only son of the widow was not lying buried in the depths of the Mediterranean after all!

I have always been more interested in persons than in places. So I shall confine what I have to say here about my time in Australia to a few remarks about a Jesuit priest I met there. We became close friends during my three years in that country. He was both a friend and a father.

The priest was Father Albert Power. How can I begin to summarise his life story? To tell it in full I would require the whole book and not be finished. His influence over me was on a par with the influence of Father George Byrne. He was rector and professor of Scripture in the seminary. What we said on the occasion of our first meeting I do not remember. What does remain in my mind is that he had a wide table in his room laden with stacks of different pamphlets written by himself. He stuffed some of them into my pockets, telling me that that was what they were for. All his life he was a prolific writer and the thought of his industry and zeal has many times encouraged me to go on writing when the temptation to drop the pen was very strong. 'I only wish', he told me, 'that I could write with both hands at the same time.' I wondered sometimes if he had not acquired that art!

He was among the first to recognise the greatness of St. Thérèse, long before she was even beatified. He was low-sized and people used actually to joke a bit about Little Flower and Little Power. A highly-placed Jesuit, who liked to pride himself on being hard-headed, explained that "we want no Little Flowers in the Society of Jesus. What we do want is *warriors*.' Somebody, not Father Power, answered quietly: 'If we had more Little Flowers in the Society we would have more warriors'.

Fidelity to grace had developed in Father Power three very lovable traits which we look for in an unspoilt little child. Little children believe without question what they are told. Tell a child the most fantastic fairy tale and he will accept it and live it all over again in his imagination. This priest had been told the most astounding 'fairy tales' by his heavenly Father. All the immense and beautiful teaching in the Church's theology he found to be enthralling. Here was a whole series of fascinating stories, and he thrilled to realise that not only were they beautiful but they were true. He had acquired a sort of sixth sense, a sense of the supernatural, which made all these stories come alive. The great mysteries of God – His power, love and mercy, His knowledge, His everlastingness – all these he had studied and prayed over, and he got up from his knees jubilant because they were true. The Blessed Eucharist, Mary, the sacraments – all true. I can almost hear him cheer, like a schoolboy dashing home in breathless excitement, to announce an unexpected prize.

This is faith, pulsating with life, not the sterile, anaemic substitute, which remains listless and unmoved in the face of such marvels. Try to taste its sweetness in a passage like the following: 'Do I realise that Jesus is pursuing me in order to catch and hold me as His own forever? He wants to fold me in His arms, to clasp me as He clasped St. John at the last supper, and to be my friend for eternity!' When the Father tells these wonderful stories, His little children sit around Him breathless, and Father Albert Power is right in the middle of them all, his eyes fixed on the Story-teller, his mind alert, his heart burning within him.

Little children love games. God's children spend all their days playing the game of seeking Him and finding Him. And where does one look for Him? The secret of Father Power's inexhaustible charity was that in every person he contacted, saint or sinner, old or young, man, woman or child, he detected the presence of Christ. One would think that to recognise Christ in this way had become second nature to him.

After Our Lord's transfiguration we read that the three men favoured with this vision, 'lifting up their eyes, saw nobody but only Jesus'. There was literally nothing that Father Albert Power would not do, for anyone, that was humanly possible. Examples abound, and the explanation lies in the fact that, in serving and helping others he 'saw no one but only Jesus'. *As long as you did it to one of these, My least brethren, you did it to Me.*

Here is a typical example. One evening he was due to travel

back to the college by train. He missed his connection and there would not be another for some hours. All that day his mind had been haunted by the thought of a woman who was very ill and had not been to the sacraments for many years. Perhaps it was not altogether a misfortune that he had missed that train. So, late at night as it already was, he undertook the long journey. He got to the nearest station but he was not familiar with the road leading from there to the woman's house. He stumbled along as best he could, and, by striking several matches, finally got there.

The dying woman gave him a cold welcome, telling him he might have spared himself the journey, as she didn't want him and she had every intention of dying as she had lived. But this persistent little priest remained there, kneeling by the bedside, with hands joined, praying aloud, and imploring the Lord, by the merits of His Sacred Passion, to touch her heart with His grace. His prayer was answered. The woman opened her eyes and struck her breast and kissed the crucifix he held to her lips. Father Albert had found Christ in a poor soul which needed Him sorely. 'You did it to Me'.

Albert Power, God's child, had a wonderful mother and he never let go of her hand. 'Mary loves God with such intense fervour', he wrote, 'that all her prayers and efforts are directed to winning others to love Him too. . . . Look upon her as a mother; trust her as a mother and expect from her the tenderness, gentleness, and compassion which experience tells us may be expected from a mother's heart. The gentlest thing on God's earth is a mother's love for her child, and through this gentle influence Jesus wins His way to our affection.

The unspoilt child is habitually happy, and Albert Power radiated happiness wherever he went. This is another trait in his childlikeness. It was founded on his vivid realisation of the mercy of God. Listen to this: 'Mortal sin is a crisis in the human soul which no mere creature can deal with. Only God's omnipotence can set things right. It is in order to supply a remedy for this and find the means of lifting fallen man from death to life, from the darkness of sin to the light of God's friendship that the Second Person of the Blessed Trinity assumed our flesh . . . His mission was, to pay the price of our redemption and to reveal to us the secret of God's infinite mercifulness to the repentant sinner'.

During the last few weeks of painful illness his joyousness increased. 'The old heart is running down', he said with a smile. 'It's about time it did, you know. It has been ticking for a long time now.' A last remark. This gentle priest, for all his gifts of affection, was no sentimentalist. He was an intellectual giant. It is only with an effort that I can refrain from writing more about him. Like him, I can say that the old heart has been ticking for a long time in me too, longer than in his case. The Little Flower said she would spend her heaven doing good upon earth. Father Power could well say the same about himself.

In him I saw the ideal Jesuit in action – hard work, supported by continuous prayer, and both vivified by a spirit of joyousness which tended to become infectious.

'Albert Power,' said Father Murtagh at his funeral, 'glowed with an immense apostolic activity. His life was a chain of grace which radiated the light and the heat and the love of God to all who knew him. I sincerely believe that it would be almost impossible to overstate the influence exercised over souls, in many parts of the world, by this diminutive priest.'

More than twenty years later I was to return to Australia. It came about in this way. From time to time our Father General in Rome sends to every Province a priest who is officially known as Father Visitor. He has a personal interview with every member of the Province to which he is assigned, from the most youthful novice to the most venerable and ancient priest or brother. Each person is encouraged to talk openly and fully about himself, his vocation, his prayer, his work, and any difficulties, complaints or suggestions he might have. This is a most wise practice.

In 1956 Father John J. McMahon, from the United States, was appointed Visitor to Australia and Ireland. He wrote to all our Houses some weeks before he was due to arrive saying that it would be a help to him if we had anything of particular interest to say, to put it briefly in writing and mail it to him so that he might have time to consider it before actually meeting the writer. I acted on his suggestion. I pointed out that I had been giving missions and retreats at home for twenty years and it occurred to me that if I returned to Australia I would have a completely new field and new audiences for the work I had been doing. When I had my talk with him, he said immediately: 'So you want to go to Australia, father?' Yes, and what did His Reverence think of the idea? His Reverence jumped at it. 'Go ahead by all means, father. They are short of men out there. Many of the Jesuits in Australia know you well. They are certain to give you a warm welcome and you will find an abundant harvest.' 'Thank you, father', I replied. 'I'll be delighted to go'. 'Fine. And for how long?' 'That is for you to say'. 'Shall we make it a year, or two years?' 'I leave that to you.' 'Right. Let's make it two.'

And two it turned out to be. I don't think I ever worked harder in my life. The demand for retreats to priests and religious and laity was incessant. I loved every moment of that time in Australia and the privilege I had of speaking about God and the things of God, in private and in public, to so many thousands of people.

After six or seven months I wrote back to my Provincial in Dublin, the late Father Charles O'Conor, to give him an account of my stewardship. I asked him please to allow me stay in Australia, or at least to consent to my extending my two years to three. He said no to both requests. I was to come back to Ireland after two years as had been arranged. Had he allowed it, I feel certain I would be in Australia till this day.

A report circulated about me after I had left home which caused reactions of surprise, incredulity, regret and alarm. It was stated that Father Nash had left the Jesuits. People who knew me well considered that I was always very 'steady' in my vocation. Had I also left the priesthood? People recalled that I had very often written of my love and admiration for the Society of Jesus. What could have happened which could cause me to abandon my vocation to it? My friend Mary Purcell was seriously interrogated by a priest who was a friend of us both, as to why I had made this move. There was, indeed, a flutter in the dovecot, but, thank God, there was not a vestige of truth in what was a mere fabrication, devised by somebody – I never knew who – with a fertile imagination.

Father O'Conor wrote to me in Australia telling me to send a letter to the *Sunday Press* 'forthwith' denying the entertaining story. I did so. The alarm bell ceased to toll. The alarmists were effectually silenced and there followed a great calm. It seems the rumour started when somebody noticed that the letters 'S.J.' were omitted in one of my articles. 'How small a fire can enkindle a great wood!'

This incident leads me to say, with deep gratitude to God and to Mary, that I never once seriously contemplated taking that step. Readers who have endured all the egoism packed into these pages so far will have detected, I hope, that in my sixty-four years with the Jesuits, I have experienced, habitually, immense peace and contentment of heart and mind. But I would not be honest if I omitted to add that this does not mean that there was not many a ripple on the surface, or even a storm brewing in the depths underneath. I have had my dark days. But I never lost sight of the fact that the sun was shining behind the dark clouds, that it would break through eventually. This always happened. Once or twice, I do remember toying with the idea of entering a Contemplative Order.

My allotted time in Australia had come and gone. On my way home I stopped off at the beautiful island of Ceylon, now known as Sri Lanka. I had been invited to give a retreat to the Jesuits there and also to the Good Shepherd Nuns and yet another to a group of native clergy. I have grateful memories of all those wonderful people and their zeal for souls. As one would expect, I felt especially at home with my Jesuit brothers. All over the Society St. Ignatius's little book of Spiritual Exercises develops principles and ideals which make us realise that we are members of one vast family. This proved to be true in Ceylon. We spoke the same language. We had the same outlook on life, the same difficulties, the same successes and failures. I was made to feel that I had known these fine priests and brothers all my life. God's grace was active in our souls during those days of prayer and silence. The whole-hearted co-operation with the message of Christ on the part of those making these retreats, however imperfectly delivered by the conductor, created an atmosphere of peace and tranquillity in which the voice of the Holy Spirit could be clearly heard.

I had a special interest in the Good Shepherd Sisters in the island. One of them, Sister Ailbe, had been in charge of groups of girls, aspirants to the Order, in New Ross in Ireland.

I had many contacts all over the country in those days, which gave me the opportunity of telling girls who might be interested, about Ceylon and New Ross. Many responded and I looked forward to meeting them again. It is understatement to say they did not regret the sacrifice made by leaving home. They felt compensated a thousand times by the opportunities opened out to them here, to work in schools and hospitals, and, most of all, in the spirit of their Mother Foundress, St. Euphrasia, to bring back to Christ poor girls who had gone astray.

Let me tell in some detail, the story of one of these sisters. I met her for the first time at St. Joseph's Retreat House, Dun Laoghaire. It was she who had organised the group, and before the retreat ended we spoke together. We talked indifferently for a short while. Then I asked her if she had ever thought of becoming a nun. She stared at me incredulously and then, leaning back in her chair she laughed. 'Me a nun father! Not at all! I'm engaged to be married.' 'Fine, that's good news and I hope and pray that you will have a happy marriage.' But Christ's invitation was there. She quotes the Hound of Heaven in telling the wonderful story of her vocation. Christ finally caught up with His quarry who had been trying desperately to escape.

She was a strong character, a born leader and organiser, a lover of innocent fun, sound in judgment, making friends easily and most important of all, filled with a deep spirit of living faith and close intimacy with Christ in prayer. Readers will be able to finish the story for themselves. Yes. She went to Sister Ailbe and New Ross, was finally professed, and here now I meet her again, as cheerful as ever, and fired with love of Jesus and Mary and zeal for souls. Only the recording angel can tell the names of the thousands of poor girls whom she has loved with a mother's love and brought back to Christ.

Her fiancé was disconsolate. He could neither sleep nor eat. But he soon discovered, of course, that she was not the only pebble on the beach.

I wrote to her some weeks ago. I told her about *My Last Book* and suggested that she might contribute a few paragraphs about her adopted country and her experiences there. Here is a portion of her reply:

As the plane taxied along the tarmac coming into Colombo airport, I could feel the scorching air and I knew I was in for a hot time. I was looking forward to coming to Ceylon and to meeting some of my Jesuit confrères and some of the Irish nuns whom I knew in their youth. It was thrilling to see those Irish eyes smiling at the barrier. The tall coconut trees, rising to some forty or fifty feet in the air, and some of them slanting at as much as a thirty degree angle, defying all the laws of gravity as it seemed to me, did not take even a stir out of that sun-drenched atmosphere. I perspired profusely in my black clerical suit. Sister sympathised and promised to provide me with a priest's light cotton cassock when we reached the convent.

The *céad mile failte* was exceedingly warm. I was to discover that the Ceylonese are a very friendly people, 'sober'n easy like ourselves', as one of our Irish Sisters described them. I saw evidence of great poverty. We traversed 'the gardens' where so many people live in overcrowded shanties. There has been considerable improvement here in recent years.

As always the nuns look out for the poor and the lowly who are in plentiful supply. They have shelters for unwed mothers, orphans, delinquents, and disturbed teenagers. They also have a sort of marriage bureau. There were up to six hundred inmates in the whole complex.

We drove to Kandy, the city of former kings of Lanka, situated about sixty miles from Colombo and over three thousand feet above sea-level. Here it was a little less scorching, with a few tea plantations on the hills away in the distance. The scenery here is breath-taking and all along the route to Kandy. High mountains on one side, paddy fields in the valleys and away in the distance to the right the famous 'Bible Rock' and on the left Saradhia Cave at Sitawaka – the Robin Hood of Lanka. The intense heat, stifling though it was, did nothing to ease the pain in a tooth of mine which was aching badly. Sister Finbarr drove me through the town to a dentist named Euroute. She made me conversant with all the historic buildings, including the Temple of the Tooth. It contains a relic of the Lord Buddha – his tooth, sacred to all devout Buddhists. This temple is of very eastern architecture, with elephants carved in stone all around the enclosure.

You will understand that my attention was divided as the tooth continued to throb. Eventually I had the disquieting member extracted and the dentist, in his kindness, held it up for my inspection. He suggested very politely that perhaps I would like him to wrap it in paper to take away with me. To Sister Finbarr's horror, I quipped: 'No, no. Not at all. You can put it in Buddha's Temple with his tooth.' I did not realise that this was grossly insulting, but light dawned as soon as I observed that Sister Finbarr left in a greaty hurry, bundling me with her.

The highlight of my journey was a visit to the wonderful Benedictine Bishop, Dr. Regno, then retired from the Kandy

Diocese, but spiritually very active among the estate workers to whom he ministered with a truly Christlike zeal. There are many stories about him which confirm this report. He shared their poverty and died, as they die, without leaving a penny to his name. There were reports about his power with God which seemed to be miraculous. His devotion to Our Lady was the joy of his life.

As I was telling that story I remembered another. The setting for this one is another Good Shepherd Convent, in Abbotsford, Melbourne. Two policemen arrived at the door one evening, conducting a young girl who had been 'committed' by the court to the care of the nuns. They deposited their charge in the convent parlour, leaving Mother Patrick to go on from there. Left alone now with the nun, she spoke for the first time, uttering these remarkable words: 'If I don't get out of this place tonight I'll smash the windows and break up the furniture!' The nun rejoined: 'Listen, child. I have something to say to you.' 'Child! How dare you call me child! I don't know who my mother was or my father for that matter.' Mother Patrick went on: 'You never had the love of a mother. I'm longing to give it to you if only you will allow me.' The nun saw the words had pierced the girl's defences, though only ever so little. 'No more nonsense now about breaking furniture. Pick up that bag of yours and come along and I'll give you a lovely supper.'

She stayed two weeks during which she sulked and insulted and screamed by turns. Not a syllable of thanks ever crossed her lips, even to Mother Patrick, who refused to be beaten. Cease fire came only when it was discovered one morning that she had disappeared off the face of the earth and was nowhere to be found. They even dredged the river Yarra, close by, but with no result.

Mother Patrick prayed perseveringly for this poor girl. Seventeen years passed and one morning she was called to the phone. 'Doctor X, here, Mother. I am calling to ask if you remember a girl named Y, who says you know her.' 'Indeed I do. Have you any news of her?' 'Yes, she is here and she is dying. We asked her if she had any friends. No, she told us sullenly. "Everyone hated me." We persisted. Then she told us "The only person who ever showed me any love was Mother Patrick of Abbotsford. If she is still living I'd like to see her before I die." ' Twenty minutes later Mother Patrick was sitting by her bedside. Both were overjoyed. They embraced – mother and child. During that seventeen years she had been, indeed, a prodigal daughter.

As tactfully as possible Mother brought up the question of the sacraments. 'No. I've finished with all that stuff long ago and I intend to die as I lived.' Of course Mother was not taking that as final. Ultimately her love and obvious anxiety prevailed. An excellent priest was summoned. The 'child' was absolved, received holy communion and Extreme Unction – now re-named the sacrament of the sick. She died a few hours later, with the priest on one side and the nun on the other, holding her beads, kissing

> the crucifix, making repeated acts of contrition, commending herself to Mary, Mother of God and Refuge of Sinners.
>
> One thought more. We may confidently hope that that girl saved her soul. Would this have happened if Mother Patrick had adopted an attitude of defiance, of threat, of harshness? The immense power of the spoken word to kill or to cure!

My own mother sometimes used to refer to the two of us as 'the only son of his mother, and she was a widow'. The words originally referred to the widow of Nalm and her son. Jesus met her one day, weeping, as she walked behind the coffin in which lay the dead body of her only son. Jesus stopped the bier, laid His hand on the coffin, told the mother to dry her tears, raised the dead boy to life and gave him back to her. We are left to imagine what must have been her ecstatic joy and her speechless amazement at what she saw and heard.

I think my own mother's happiness cannot have been much less when, back from Australia, I stepped out of the train at Limerick, where, she was waiting for me.

I was glad also to be back in Milltown Park, because of what it now stood for in my life. I was about to face four years of theology and at the end of the third year would come my ordination to the priesthood. Long ago I had told Father Murphy, the Redemptorist, that I had never wanted to be anything but a priest. The only change during that lengthy interval was that, if possible, the desire had deepened. And now the goal was well in sight.

I gave much thought and prayer to the vocation of a priest and all it implies, during those three years. My study of theology helped to expand my view and to increase my understanding of the sublimity and responsibility of the way of life which lay before me. I read much about the priesthood, finding inspiration, among others, in Archbishop Fulton Sheen's enthralling book *The Priest is not His Own.*

Much light and encouragement came to me also from the guidance and example of the older priests who had persevered so faithfully in this way of life. I recall especially Father Henry Fagan. If you asked him, when in his eighties, how he was, his eyes would shine and he would answer, invariably: 'How am I? Leppin', leppin', thank God.' I know another octogenarian who is still 'leppin', thank God', feeling at 82 like 28.

4 A Priest Forever

The thoughts which formed in my mind over sixty years ago about the priest's vocation are as fresh there today as they were then. I hope I have never lost sight of the ideal, however poorly I may have lived it out. Our Holy Father, John Paul II, has developed the meaning of that ideal in as complete a manner as possible, leaving no aspect untouched. It is a great consolation to me to discover, that I, in my own small way, have talked in many retreats to priests and clerics, along the same lines. One explanation of this may be that the Holy Father, over the years, may have slipped unobtrusively into some of my talks, incorporated what he listened to from behind the door into his writings and addresses, and passed them off as his own! Seriously, I would like to say that all the Pope's teaching on the priesthood has been brought together in a neat volume by Father Seamus O'Byrne, to whom we are deeply indebted. His book, entitled *A Priest Forever*, can be got from St. Paul's Publications, Athlone (price £2.50).

I felt, first of all, a sense of grave responsibility in preparing to accept the ideals of the priesthood. I read, carefully and repeatedly, Pius XII's weighty words of warning to seminarians and their spiritual directors. Every aspirant should receive adequate training and instruction, and, if there be a serious doubt about his fitness, he should be dismissed, gently but firmly. To allow him to remain, out of sympathy for himself or his relatives is a false charity which may well lead to great trials and difficulties. Pope St. Pius X had said earlier: 'A holy priest makes holy people. A priest who is not holy is not only useless, but harmful to the world'. Pius XI also wrote: 'If the Church has a holy and a learned priesthood she has nothing to fear from her enemies. But if she does not have that, any other advantage she may seem to have will profit her little'.

On the day of ordination, at a given point, the ceremony is interrupted and the President or Rector presents to the bishop the group to be ordained, calling each one by name. He is solemnly charged to speak according to the dictates of his conscience, and voice, even now, at this eleventh hour, any serious objection he may have to any candidate. The bishop, having interrogated him, then turns to the other priests and to the entire congregation to put to them the same question. Then, and only then, is he permitted to proceed with the ceremony. At this stage the aspirants prostrate themselves flat on the floor in a semi-circle around the altar – a most impressive sight. When I had got that far I remember, to this day, heaving a sigh of relief. I was allowed to advance, thanks be to God.

Generally this interrogation is only a matter of form. But not always. A priest told me that once at this point somebody in the congregation stood up and announced that he objected to one of the candidates being allowed to go on for ordination. There was consternation. The bishop had no choice but to interrupt the ceremony and take the unhappy man into the sacristy. His ordination was postponed. Please don't ask me why the objector handled the situation in such a clumsy way. The priest who told me the story assured me that he was present and saw and heard the entire unhappy episode.

'As bishop of Rochester', Archbishop Sheen tells us, 'I rejected a few deacons who were presented to me for ordination. I had felt when examining them, and also from observing them in the seminary when I made visits, that their intentions were not worthy. When the news finally got around concerning the rejection of certain members of the class, a mother of one of the young men came to me and said: 'Thank God you are not ordaining my son. He is not worthy to be a priest'. Several other members of the class came to me and said: 'How did you know? Your judgement was right'.

I was ordained a Jesuit priest on 31 July 1931, feast of St. Ignatius, by Bishop Francis Wall. There were twelve in our group, and, as far as I can find out, I am the only survivor. It has always seemed to me that this most moving ceremony was beautifully foreshadowed in a gospel scene which is described by three of the four evangelists.

Jesus would seem to have spent a considerable amount of

time on the previous evening arguing with His enemies and failing to convince them. Their hearts were embittered with pride and the living word of God could not penetrate through the hard core of obstinacy. He sent them away, sorrowful. He dismissed also those persons who had taken his message to heart, and these included the twelve apostles whom He would call to Himself in a special manner in the morning. All alone now, as He wanted to be, Jesus sought strength and consolation in communicating with His Father in prayer. With eyes now shut and now lifted up He knelt there 'and He spent the whole night in the prayer of God, Himself alone'. What depths of thought for meditation are contained in this simple statement. In another place we shall see that Jesus is, first and before all else, a man of prayer, and that He seems to have a predilection for prayer in private, plunged in His contemplation of the mysteries of God.

On this particular occasion He prays all the night through because on the morrow He has a work to do which will be of vast importance for His Church. He would teach us by His example to pray fervently for light to do what is right in God's sight. In every important decision to be made – about a proposal for marriage, about a job to be accepted or not – the question of primary importance always must be: 'What does God want me to do?' The task awaiting Jesus in the morning is the selection of His first twelve priests. In another place we learn that the mission He wants to entrust to them is threefold: to be with Him, to preach, to cast out devils. He spent all the night in this aloneness, His whole being steeped in God. We could do nothing better than imitate Him.

As soon as the first rays of morning begin to break through in the eastern sky Jesus rises from His knees and proceeds to walk down the slope of the mountain. The crowds have come back, unable to resist the attractiveness of this man. It was a large gathering, thousands, perhaps. Standing there a little elevated above them on the slope He holds them with a gesture, raising both arms full, to indicate that they are to keep their distance for the present. From this point of vantage He looks down the centre. He looks over to the right and over to the left. He has decided on the twelve precise men He wants and no one else will do. Peter, Andrew, James and John –

each is His special choice. Not this one, nor that one, but the man standing between, 'whom He would Himself', we learn. Each one of the twelve, called by name, leaves his place and takes up his position beside his Master and Lord.

By a happy coincidence there were twelve of us in the group at Milltown Park on that eventful morning. We knelt around the altar in a semi-circle, each of us in a white alb, and our Rector, the late Father Cyril Power presented us to the bishop, requesting him, for the good of the Church, to raise each one of us to the priesthood. 'Do you consider them to be worthy?' the bishop asked. 'Yes. In so far as I am able to judge, and making allowances for human frailty, it is my considered opinion that they are worthy'. 'Thanks be to God'.

Then, just as Jesus called each one of His first priests by name, so was each one of us called: 'Joseph, John, Robert, Timothy . . .' In due course we received the power to consecrate the bread and wine into the body and blood of Christ in the Mass; to absolve from sin; to bless and to preach. After more than fifty years the memory is still fresh in my mind.

After the ceremony came our blessings to be given as priests. Each of us stood by a prie-dieu, fully vested as priests for the first time, and each of our friends and relatives came up and knelt in turn. First in my queue was my mother. She knelt and bowed her head and I signed her with the sign of the cross, and, laying my hands – with the oil scarcely dry on them as yet – on her bowed head I invoked God's blessing upon her. Canon John Rea, a very close friend of both of us, from Limerick, bent down over her and whispered: 'My warm congratulations. You have been many years waiting for this moment'.

Half an hour later each of us newly-ordained priests sat at a special table reserved for each group, having breakfast, radiantly happy. In the afternoon we adjourned to a very modest hotel where we enjoyed a very adequate but very simple lunch. Luxurious festivities and swell parties tend to create an atmosphere in which the spiritual joy seems easily to rub off.

On the following morning I said my first Mass in the convent of Our Lady of Charity of Refuge in Sean McDermott

Street. I heard a priest say in a retreat lecture: 'Fathers, you will preach your most effective sermon, for Christ or against Him, according as you celebrate your Mass with or without devotion and reverence'. I said to a fairly young priest lately: 'Father, congratulations on the way in which you have just said your Mass. If every priest said Mass like you, ninety per cent of the troubles regarding the Mass would disappear overnight, because people would know what the Mass is'.

At his ordination a priest is consecrated forever to Christ and His Church. What does this mean? A church is consecrated, when the building is set aside, absolutely and forever, exclusively, for the worship of God. So it may never be lawfully used for any other purpose. Not every church is consecrated in this way. In this case, in the course of years, it may be altered and used for some other purpose – as a lecture-room or theatre – but *never* if it has been consecrated. It remains God's exclusive property forever.

A chalice is consecrated and so it may never lawfully be used for any purpose except to contain Christ's Precious Blood. It would be desecration to put it on the breakfast table and drink tea or coffee from it. King Baltasser, in the Old Testament, did something like this. He took the sacred vessels which belonged to the temple, 'and the king sat and his nobles, and his wives and his concubines' and drank from these sacred cups. A hand appeared writing on the wall, expressive of God's anger, 'and the king's countenance changed and his thoughts troubled him, and his knees struck, one against the other'. As well they might. He had desecrated what was sacred.

The ordained priest no longer belongs to himself; he is God's exclusive property. All other ways of life are trespassers on holy ground, to be ruthlessly prosecuted. They are like the buyers and the sellers who turned God's consecrated temple into a den of thieves. Christ could not endure such insolence. He was furious. He made a whip and drove those trespassers out, in headlong confusion, turning their tables upside-down and warning them of the gravity of their sin.

This inner seal, stamped on the priest's heart and marking it as Christ's very own, will manifest itself exteriorly. At the Transfiguration on Tabor Christ allowed the rays of the divinity to penetrate through the veils of the humanity. It was only a flash, but the three men privileged to witness it wanted to remain forever, gazing into its splendour, never any more going back to the drab valleys down below.

In some such way the priest must radiate Christ, in everything he does and says and thinks. A picture flung on the screen may be blurred because it is out of focus. But, according as the operator adjusts the lens, the image becomes clearer and ultimately the full picture is reproduced, perfect in every detail. Every new day, upon which the consecrated priest embarks, he will be concerned to adjust the focus, striving towards the ideal which would allow men, like those on Tabor, to see in him 'no one but only Jesus'.

The priest, then, will do the things which Jesus did. Christ preached, and the people said: 'Never did man speak as this man speaks'. The priest does not need to be an intellectual or a great orator. The Curé of Ars was neither and he drew the whole world after him, because people discerned in his faulty sentences the unmistakable echo of his Master's voice. A priest asked a very successful actor: 'How does it come about that you can draw the crowds and so often we priests fail to do so?' 'Father', he was told, 'we actors speak fiction as if it was fact, and you priests speak fact as if it was fiction'. St. Stephen's enemies 'were not able to resist *the Spirit that spoke in him*'. And Christ reminded His first priests 'It is not you who speak, but the Spirit of your Father who speaks in you'.

Jesus came, not to condemn but to forgive. In the years preceding ordination I often looked forward to the day when I would be consecrated to do the same. Our Lord sat by the well of Jacob on a hot day in summer. He was 'weary from His journey'. A poor sinful woman came to the well to draw water. He knew she would be coming. He was waiting for her to come. He transformed her into an apostle. St. John tells us the thrilling story in the fourth chapter of his gospel. It is a perfect setting for the priest, perhaps weary too, waiting there in the confessional for sinners, to work miracles of conversion in their souls, through the power given him at ordination. We read of miracles, physical miracles, at Lourdes and elsewhere, but they pale into insignificance before the miracles of grace worked in this sacrament. Someone has written: 'Devotion to the work of hearing confessions is an infallible mark of the true priest'.

Jesus offered Himself as a victim for sin on the cross. The priest not only offers the Mass. He offers himself as a victim of love in union with Christ who did the same before him. This theme is inspiringly developed by Archbishop Sheen in his book *The Priest is not His Own*. What a wealth of thought in all these considerations, waiting to be discovered! The priest does not say: 'This is the Body of Christ. This is the blood of Christ'. What he does say is: 'This is *MY* body. This is *MY* blood'. He does not say: 'Christ forgives you your sins', but '*I* forgive you your sins'. It is an overpowering thought that the priest can truly speak like this, because, by virtue of his consecration, to his frail keeping have been entrusted powers which belong by right only to God.

This consecration affects the life of the priest not only when he is performing duties proper to the priesthood, but also in his ordinary relations with other people. I have always liked to think of Christ as He walks among men in the ordinary ways, interested in their problems, partaking of their ordinary pleasures and accepting their hospitality. Thus He called Zachaeus down from the tree and invited Himself to a meal in his house. And we learn that they had 'a great feast'. He was a guest at the marriage feast of Cana and, at the suggestion of His Mother, He worked His first public miracle there. Martha and Mary loved Him very much and served His lunch with perfect courtesy, and if these two sisters were like so many of the kindly women of our day, we can be sure that the food was excellent. He was thirsty and He asked for a drink. He was weary and He sat down to rest. He was exhausted and He stretched out His tired body in Peter's boat and fell fast asleep. And let me not fail to notice that He put a pillow under His head. I often thank Him for that pillow and hope that I am not too self-indulgent when I accept gratefully from Him the pillow with which He supplies me every night.

What I am trying to show here is that our consecration is all-embracing. 'Whether you eat or whether you drink or whatever else you do, do all to the glory of God'. Christ does not at all frown on the good priest or layman who has schooled himself to use the gifts given him in the natural order, with moderation and as a means to a worthy end.

A last word about this imitation of Christ. It differs widely from the efforts of a young man who is anxious to be an author and models his writing on the style of somebody who has attained eminence in this field. It is not like the attempt of the schoolboy, keen on sport, who studies the technique of the captain of the college. The priest's assimilation consists, above all, in reproducing the mind and heart of Christ. 'Let this *mind* be in you', writes St. Paul, 'which also was in Christ Jesus'. The exterior imitation of Christ must be vivified by the life of grace within his soul.

This basic truth concerning the consecration of the priest is admirably expressed by Father Molinari S.J. in *The Way*, for September 1971.

> If we do not learn Christ interiorly, if we do not know Him as St. Paul and St. Peter knew Him – and the other apostles – we shall betray our mission, which is simply His. We shall preach nothing but ourselves. . . . Apostolic activity requires in the apostle *interior dispositions*, which are to be found only in those who, like the Twelve, have sat for a long time at the feet of the Lord and have listened to His word. In silence and in prayer they have become men who are willing to take up their cross and follow Him unconditionally, supported by a love which is stronger than themselves.

This theme I find so fascinating that, although I have devoted a considerable amount of space to it, I am the first to confess that the treatment is inadequate and scrappy. What I have written, even thus faultily presented, must justify the statement that the ideal put before the priest is the highest possible towards which human nature, aided by a powerful grace, can aspire. Pope John Paul II summarises, in his usual forthright manner, what I have been trying to say.

> Reflect on your identity. You have been called, elected by Jesus Himself, the divine Master and Saviour of our souls, the Redeemer of men. He has chosen you, in a mysterious but real way, to make you saviours with Him and like Him; He wants *to change you into Himself*; to entrust to you His own divine powers. To succeed in your intention hand yourselves over to the Blessed Virgin Mary, always, but especially in moments of difficulty and darkness. From Mary we learn to surrender to God's Will in all things. From Mary we learn to trust, even when all hope seems gone. From Mary we learn to love Christ, her Son and the Son of God.

The following words, attributed to Saint Teresa, are relevant here:

> Christ has now no body on earth but yours; no hands but yours; no feet but yours. Yours are the eyes through which Christ's compassion for the world is to look out. Yours are the feet with which He is to go about doing good. Yours are the hands with which He is to bless men today.

And this applies, not only to priests and religious, but to all our Catholic laity, as is abundantly clear from the teaching of Vatican II.

I have allowed my pen to run freely on this theme, because, let me confess it, I have a deep affection for my brother-priests. I have been privileged to meet thousands of them in retreats and parish missions and in social life. Four of the books I managed to get through the press have been written primarily for them. *The Priest at his Prie-dieu*, *The Seminarian at his Prie-dieu*, *Ten Priests* and *Ten More Priests*. Once, when I was going to Rome, my brethren spread the impish story that the object of my visit was to collect material for a new book, *The Pope at his Prie-dieu*.

Do all priests succeed in striving all their lives towards the ideal I have been trying to describe? Human nature being what it is, nobody can be surprised that some do gradually lower that ideal and finally lose sight of it altogether. If the spotlight is played exclusively on the laicised priest regrettable results are likely to follow. Lay people could easily become confused and doubtful, or even sceptical and cynical. There are Catholics who have lapsed because, as they allege, they have encountered priests who were tyrants or hypocrites. For these the story of the priest who leaves is grist for the mill.

Too much stress on these cases could sow the seeds of doubt and anxiety in the mind of a young man contemplating this vocation. He may well have in him the potential to do for God and souls a work comparable to that of St. Francis Xavier or the Curé of Ars. All these years it has been plain sailing. But now? There is X, a model student in the seminary, and he lasted only two years after ordination. There is Y, who gave up only three months before he was due to take the final step. There are intellectuals and theologians who serve us up with arguments why they cannot accept the Church's teaching. Small wonder if the poor lad is bewildered!

Again. Isn't it fair to suggest that the one-sided view could add enormously to the problem of a priest, who, perhaps has begun to waver? He is shocked to discover priests who share, it seems, his doubts, but not his anxiety. They talk about the move they are contemplating almost like a layman discussing a proposed change of job.

This is not a pleasant subject, I confess, but the fact that many priests leave, cannot be swept under the carpet. It is our hope and prayer that priests and students and laity who are distressed by this state of affairs may be comforted and encouraged by what I have written on earlier pages concerning the meaning and sublimity and joy of the true priest.

'The true priestly spirit is acquired', writes Canon Ripley, 'not so much by books and study as in the sanctuary. Where the Heart of Christ beats, there is the school of the true apostolate. It was on the breast and on the heart of Jesus that John became the beloved disciple'.

What about the Jesuits? It would be foolish and false to deny that we too have suffered in this way. It is anguish to admit this, especially as one has come to love the Ignatian ideal and sees it being cast aside. Not for us to judge or question motives. Whatever these may be, the actual fact, considered in itself, can cause nothing but deep sorrow and sincere sympathy.

And then, of course, there is the bright side. If there is shadow on one side of the hedge there is brilliant sunshine on the other. Father James Brodrick, biographer of the Jesuit, St. Peter Canisius, writes, quoting the saint: 'The more afflicted and desperate things are in the world's opinion, the more will it be our part to come to the rescue of forlorn hopes, precisely because we belong to the Society of Jesus'. That 'precisely because', adds Father Broderick, 'should make a Jesuit's blood tingle like the music of trumpets'.

And, thank God, it does. Having lived with the Jesuits for more than sixty years, I can truthfully state that I have long since lost count of the number of men, priests and brothers and students, whose dedication to Christ, to the Mother of God, to the Church and to souls, fills me, not only with wonder, but with awe and a holy envy. In their daily lives, they laid bare, day after day, a soul and a heart and a mind, which had accepted unreservedly, the sound spiritual principles bequeathed to them by St. Ignatius.

I feel strongly urged, at this point, to select one or two Jesuits and set out by way of illustration, a brief account of the lives they lived. One of my closest friends in the Society for many years was the late Father John MacSheahan. For most of his life he suffered acutely and continually, but no one ever heard a syllable of complaint from his lips, or saw a gesture of impatience or any sign of self-pity. Indeed his consistent good-humour was infectious.

'How are you, Father John?' I asked him one day. I had not seen him for some months and it was with a shock amounting to horror that I noted the change in his appearance. We met on the stairs. He stood there before me extending his hand in welcome. I can see him at this moment, gaunt, slightly stooped, wan and wrinkled and emaciated, and wearing black glasses, crooked on his nose.

'How am I? Sure I'm fine', he said trying to adjust the spectacles. 'Of course, you heard, I suppose, that I've lost the sight of this eye and the hearing of this ear'. He indicated both, covering each in turn, for a moment with his open palm. 'Then the old "tummy" gives me a lot of trouble. If only I could go on living without having to take food! And all the time the noises go on in my old head'. 'Have you got them at this moment?' 'At this moment, Father Robert', and he drew his hand across his forehead, 'at this moment there is a throbbing up here like an engine. But otherwise I'm fine!'

'Otherwise I'm fine'. That, I think, sounds the characteristic note of his whole life. There was a courage and a devotion to duty, sustained heroically to the end, in spite of fearful odds, which might be called sublime. He cut the interview short. 'I shouldn't be talking about myself, you know', he said with a grin, 'but you asked for it'. That same evening he sat with the rest of us at recreation, laughing and joking and 'leg-pulling', and telling amusing stories in his own inimitable way, as though he did not have a care in the world. Who would suspect the effort it cost him daily, almost hourly, extending over his entire life – for he was never robust, even as a boy – which this habitual cheerfulness demanded? It called for even more heroic courage as the end approached. What I have written, even so far, fills me with reverence.

This man of indomitable will sat one day in his room talking to me. Suddenly, he broke down completely. His head sunk low into his hands and he gave full vent to his feelings, weeping freely. 'It's not easy going. Life is so lonely and seems so useless. I only wish the good Lord would take me altogether or else give me some help or relief'. But at once he gripped himself, apologised to me and by the end of the interview he was back again to his old self, with the familiar patient smile. But the incident was highly instructive and revealing. It gave an inkling of the depths of depression and sorrow that must often have crushed his generous heart and nearly overpowered him. But nobody knew.

On one occasion he walked into a convent to give a weekend retreat. There was an opening lecture that night, followed by confessions. On the Sunday he had four lectures, a public Holy Hour, and confessions for most of the time in-between. He looked ghastly. With those pale sunken cheeks he seemed more like a ghost than a living man. Yet he threw himself heart and soul into that strenuous programme of work and conducted the Holy Hour with such fervour that his voice could be heard outside, on the other side of the street. But again how few realised all it cost him! During the entire weekend he could take practically no food; was sick continually. Still, on the Monday morning he walked out the door with his head erect and smiling all round – and went straight into hospital for a major operation!

His optimism was irrepressible. He would tell you, with delightful simplicity, of a novena he had started to Our Lady to ask for a cure or at least some relief, and he would ask you to join in it. And when the novena came and went and nothing happened, he would brace himself to grin and carry on. He was in high glee when the Eucharistic Fast was mitigated. He could now have a cup of coffee in the early morning, and 'I can't tell you what a help it is to me in saying Mass. I don't know myself'.

No man appreciated an act of kindness more, no matter how small, a letter, a visit, a promise of prayer, or a little gift. Once he had been lamenting to Father O'Grady, his Provincial, that he was 'so useless to the Society and such an expense'. He was emphatically assured on both points. He would love to tell you the exact words which had been used to convey this truth, and the tone of voice in which they had been spoken. Clearly he treasured them with abiding gratitude.

Often when returning home from some errand of mercy he would collapse in the street with a 'black-out'. Such incidents never deterred him. He would joke about them afterwards and expatiate on as many of the details as he could recall. There was the day when he fell off his bicycle and wakened up lying on a couch in the house of a Protestant doctor. The good doctor at first had his doubts about the reason for the fall but made profound apologies and explanations when he learned the truth.

He enjoyed particularly describing his recovery after a 'black-out' when he began to realise slowly that he was somewhere in bed. He opened his eyes and, to his astonishment, saw that he was surrounded by lighted candles. This time, he said to himself, they must be convinced that I really am dead. He wondered vaguely if they might not be right! 'I'm not dead yet, am I?' he muttered to a friend standing close by. He wasn't. The electric light had failed. That was all. 'When you have been posted up among the missing as apparently dead, passed by on the operating table as presumably dead, picked up off the street for a post mortem examination, and laid out with lighted candles around your bed, you naturally begin to wonder if you are still in the land of the living at all!'

He had been ordained a little before his time in order to give him opportunity to enlist as a chaplain in the war. As always when there was question of his own virtues he was very reticent and unwilling to talk. But there is indisputable evidence of his courage in the fact that he was awarded the Military Cross twice over. Regretfully, we have to pass over the story of his career as a military chaplain.

In his last illness I had the privilege of visiting him several times. He was suffering acutely, but there was always, as usual, the bright smile of welcome. As we said goodbye on the last of these occasions, he whispered hoarsely: 'My two sisters are coming here tonight and I am also to have another visitor. So we'll have four for a game of bridge!' Two days later he was dead.

He was one of the many Jesuits who 'fill me with awe and a holy envy'. His noble life I find to be an inspiration, but also a challenge, a reproach, and an indictment.

Father Patrick Doherty once confided to a friend: 'When I stand at the altar for Mass, particularly after the Consecration, I am so overwhelmed by the thought of what has just happened, right there under my very eyes, that I feel inclined almost to look down and see if my feet are touching the ground at all.'

This deep spirit of faith developed with the years and reached its climax during his last illness. To visit him then and pray with him was an inspiration. He was radiantly happy at the prospect of the near approach of God and eternity. He often times assured us that he would change places with no one in the whole world.

A message was brought to him from his little niece, aged six. She had offered Mass and Holy Communion for Uncle Paddy and all the children in several schools were praying for him too. He was delighted, but presently his expression clouded and changed to a look of genuine alarm. 'I hope they aren't asking for a miracle, are they?' A deep friendship existed between us, and that is one reason why I felt impelled to choose him from many other Jesuits, to illustrate the Jesuit ideal in practice. I hinted to him that I had been asked to write his obituary notice. He sat up in the bed, seized both my hands with his, and looking me straight into my eyes, he said: 'Tell them I am the greatest proof of the mercy of God you ever came across'.

When his aged mother came to see him he twitted her. 'Mother dear, just imagine you fretting! What's all the fuss about anyway? Sure you'll probably be on the next old bus after me yourself. All I am going to do is move on a little ahead and open the gate and keep it open for you till you arrive and drive through'. Again: 'God is amazingly generous to us towards the end of life. No matter what the dying person thinks about himself and his sins, all the Lord seems to want now is that He wishes him to be His friend'.

Indeed, he 'opened the gate' to many a soul. So many memories of him are packed into his last few weeks on earth that there is a danger lest they obscure the years preceding. All his life long he had been something of an *enfant terrible*. As a youngster he was constantly in hot water over some boyish prank or escapade. 'He never opened a gate', says his mother. 'He would always vault it or climb over it'. Once on a time his younger brother presented himself as a candidate for the privilege of becoming a Mass server. He was one of several and he was the only one rejected. The sacristan, on hearing that he was brother to the subject of these paragraphs, preemptorily dismissed him. 'Brother, indeed, to that young scamp who had been discovered the other day climbing the roof of the church! A miracle he had escaped!'

I am tempted to let my pen run on and cover several pages with accounts of his apostolic work. There is plenty to write about, but, frankly, I am a little afraid lest some readers might consider I am indulging in fulsome praise – of him and of the Society of Jesus in general. To forestall this criticism I freely confess that, given our training, many of us show poor enough results. This is said in no spirit of harsh criticism but only to keep the record straight. True, we have thirty-eight Jesuits canonised, and several hundreds whose Cause has been introduced, and in many of these the candidates have been beatified. But, as in the history of the Church itself, there have been failures, some more serious than others, and all of them pointing to the truth that we are men, not angels, with feet of clay.

During his life he possessed in large measure the gift of genuine sympathy. The trials and sorrows and difficulties and problems of others poured in over him, causing him actual personal anxiety. He was dedicated to the apostolate of the confessional. He was a writer, and was severely critical of anything he wrote. He did splendid work for many years for the Pioneer Association of the Sacred Heart, and founded it in Australia. He was much sought after as a retreat-giver. With all this he remained to the end very human. In his last illness he admitted: 'I had always to force myself to work. It's wonderful not to have to work any more'.

He kept his mischievous sense of humour right up to the end. One day he went for a little walk along the corridor in the hospital. He needed two people, one on each side, to support him, leaning an arm over each shoulder. He came out from his room aided by a Jesuit colleague, Father Shuley, but he required a second person to help him. Nobody was in sight except a very pretty little nurse. Smilingly she offered her help. Father Doherty put one arm around the shoulder of the priest on his right, and the other around the shoulder of the girl. Then, with a twinkle in his eye, he said: 'I don't know what Father Nash would say to this!'

He had a very deep faith. He combined with his cheerfulness an ardent love of the Sacred Heart and Mary. He was surely a man of prayer. He was a great favourite with the older priests and brothers in his community. He was generous in the tributes he paid to those who had borne the labours and heat of the day. His youthful ways endeared him to young people in his Order and outside. It is hardly possible that St. Peter refused to open the gate for him.

He was fifty-one when the end came. I'll be glad indeed to meet him again and mind you, I think he'll be glad to meet me too.

May he rest in peace!

There is a third Jesuit whose name I cannot pass over in silence. I know him only from his books. God willing, maybe I will have the privilege of meeting him in person before I die. His name is Father Walter J. Ciszek, and he lives in New York. He spent twenty-three years in the Soviet Union and most of that time in prison or in the slave labour camps of Siberia. He told his story in two books *With God in Russia*, and *He Leadeth Me*. He prefers the second one. I have read it cover to cover twice over. I shall probably read it again. I have loaned my copy to others and recommended it strongly in many places. A brother Jesuit of mine read it, lent it, but the demand for it was so great that he got six copies and keeps them all rotating from one friend of his to another.

If ever there was a Jesuit priest who radiated the ideal, to a degree which might seem almost miraculous, it was Father Ciszek. I propose simply to turn over some pages with my readers and let them speak for themselves. [The book can be had from: A.R. Mowbray & Co. Ltd., St. Thomas House, Becket Street, Oxford, England].

> In the years I spent in the Siberian camps we built whole towns, constructed huge factory complexes, opened up and worked new mines, and completed all facilities necessary, to turn a frozen, barren wilderness into a functioning and productive centre of

industry. And we did it while living in the most primitive conditions, fed at starvation level, without anything but the most essential tools. We did it by forced labour, brute strength and sheer weight of numbers . . . I was assigned the lowest work and the roughest brigades. That was my lot because of the charges I had been convicted on . . . I had opportunity to work again in some fashion as a priest. When I refused to stop I was punished by being assigned to the hardest types of labour . . . doing the dirtiest work . . .

I worked to the limit of my strength each day and did as much as my health and endurance under the circumstances made possible. Why? Because I saw this work as the Will of God for me. I didn't build a new city in Siberia because Joseph Stalin or Nikita Khrushehev wanted it, but because God wanted it . . . I could not, therefore, look upon this work as degrading; it was ennobling, because it came to me from the Hand of God Himself . . .

Sometimes I think that those who have never been deprived of an opportunity to say or hear Mass do not really appreciate what the Mass is. I know, in any event, what it came to mean to me and the other priests I met in the Soviet Union. I know the sacrifices we made and the risks we ran in order to have a chance to hear or say Mass. When we were constantly hungry in the camps, when the food we got each day was barely enough to keep us going, I have seen priests pass up breakfast and work at hard labour on an empty stomach until noon, in order to keep the Eucharistic Fast, because the noon break at the work site was the time that we could best get together for a hidden Mass . . . Or again, during the long artic summer, when the work days were the longest and our hours of sleep were at a minimum, I have seen priests and prisoners deprive their bodies of needed sleep in order to get up before the rising bell for a secret Mass in a quiet barracks. We had a catacomb existence. We would be severely punished if we were discovered and there were always informers. But the Mass to us was always worth the danger and the sacrifice.

May I be allowed to round off the description of the Jesuit ideal with a very gracious quote from the celebrated Dominican, Father Thomas Burke?

'To purge out all that is base in man, to give him entire dominion over his senses and appetites, to raise his mind to loftiest thoughts and fill his soul with highest aspirations, to form his will in accordance with the noblest motives and purposes; all this is not to destroy his individual character or personality but to develop and elevate it.'

'And if in this process a number of men conform themselves to some high type of excellence, so as to become like each other in their common likeness to their type of model, this is not destroying that individuality which is sacred and must be respected, but

> rather directing its powers and shaping it to the highest and fairest.'
>
> 'Well did St. Ignatius know this, and while destroying in his children all that was imperfect and base, he most carefully respected and reverently fostered the personal character and gifts of each man, so that in no Order in the Church is there a greater freedom and diversity of personal character, nor a wider application and development of natural gifts than in the Society of Jesus'.

Having finished four years in Milltown Park, I was sent, with some of my colleagues, to St. Beono's College, North Wales, for 'Tertianship' lasting ten months. The regime was similar in many ways to what we had had as novices. St. Ignatius realised that in the interval the pressure of external work might have affected our prayer-life adversely. So he prescribed the tertianship as a period of withdrawal from the active apostolate so as to concentrate on serious reflection and the life of prayer. These ten months were intended to confirm us in our determination to become men steeped in the spirit of prayer. Cost what it may no amount of external work, even when people regard it as a success, can compensate for the absolute need of striving, all through life, to maintain this proportion. Without this, life becomes like a body without a soul.

Preaching, St. Thomas tells us in a neatly turned Latin phrase, means 'contemplari et contemplata aliis tradere', to pray, and to pass on to others the fruit of our prayer. Preaching, therefore, is the over-flowing of our prayer-life and by no means a substitute for it. It was during his tertianship that Father William Doyle was confirmed in his resolution to become a saint. Tranquillity and solitude, if they are cheerfully accepted, do much to restore the balance.

Our guide and director during this important time was Father Joseph Bolland, to whom I have ever since felt deeply grateful. He was dedicated to us, heart and soul. He presented to us, especially during the Thirty-Day-Retreat, dynamic meditations, which obviously he had made his own, in theory and practice. He told us 'to be afraid of an easy life', a phrase of his which has always stuck in my mind and which seems to me more relevant than ever in our permissive society.

I quoted it once for a fairly 'mod' Jesuit. He nearly jumped on me. 'Not at all! The thing is to be yourself'. My impression has always been that St. Ignatius urged us to 'conquer self' –

insinuating this into the very title of his Spiritual Exercises, and coming back on it several times.

I saw, more clearly than ever, the vast spiritual treasure of light and encouragement which was being offered to me. I once suggested in the *Sunday Press* that if the Reverend Ian Paisley could be induced to make the 'Spiritual Exercises' he might find himself knocking at our halldoor and asking to be admitted as a Jesuit novice! I haven't heard if he came. I must make enquiries.

During Lent we tertians were allowed to undertake some work in the active apostleship, by way of testing our wings. My assignment was as partner with the late Father Charlie Molony, universally loved inside the Society and outside. We were to give a fortnight's mission in Lurgan and a second fortnight in Belfast. Father Charlie wrote to me while I was still in Wales: 'You may as well know that I used some gentle persuasion with the chief – Father Mackey – to ask him to let me have you'. After tertianship our Father Provincial assigned me as a permanent member of the Mission and Retreat Staff and on the staff I remained for almost thirty years.

Let me set down, briefly, two experiences I had. Very early on the staff I made the acquaintance of a young man between whom and myself a close friendship was formed. It lasts to this day. His was, and is, a real faith, throbbing with life. Under direction he tried his vocation in the most austere Order in the Church, the Carthusians. He did not stay but he often told me afterwards that he thanked God for learning by experience that there were in the Church lives of such complete dedication to God. The only weekday Mass in his town was at 7.20, and he had to cycle two miles to be at his job by eight. So he forgot his breakfast every morning in order to get daily Mass and Holy Communion. He was, and is, an ardent lay apostle, speaks out fearlessly and convincingly during the lunch hour if there is smutty talk or an attack on the Church. His fellow-workers feel they cannot but admire and respect him.

Another close friend of mine was a very lovable character whom I shall call Tim. It wasn't his name. He approached me late on a Saturday night, at the close of a mission for men, just as I was leaving the confessional. I had been there eight or nine hours and could scarcely stand up straight. Neither could poor Tim! 'I want to take the pledge, father,' he told me in a thick tone of voice. 'You're not fit to take any pledge in your present condition, Tim', I answered. 'Come back in the morning when you are sober, and I'll gladly give you the pledge'. 'I'm not leaving this church tonight until I get the pledge'. So I agreed, with mixed motives, I fear, to give it to him.

We went into the parlour and Tim knelt before the crucifix, and, with hands joined, solemnly promised the Lord 'never to touch it again'. He stumbled a few times after that but finally made the grade. The climax was on his deathbed. The priest said: 'You know, Tim, you are very weak and a few drops of brandy might revive you'. 'Don't ask me, father. I made that promise in honour of the Sacred Heart sixteen years ago and I want to die keeping it.' He was the proudest man in Dublin the day he 'got the pin'. If I forget mine when I meet him in heaven I'm sure he will order me back to earth to get it and fasten it into the lapel of my coat. He said to me: 'You know, father, the way to say it is that before I met you I was never sober!'

However, some time before I was assigned, I had a very pleasant interview with our Provincial, Father Laurence Kieran. I had scarcely sat down in his room when he said: 'I suppose, Father Nash, you would like to know what we propose to do with you after tertianship. Well, I can tell you at least this much. You can take it for certain that you won't be leaving Ireland. I've come to this decision out of regard for the position of your good mother. I don't know what your work will be but you won't be leaving Ireland'. I thanked him, I was much moved by his thoughtfulness, but I was also slightly uneasy. During tertianship I had given much thought and prayer, especially during the more recent months, to ask the Lord to let me see if I should volunteer for some foreign mission. And here was the decision made for me and offered to me on a plate. Since then I have spoken from time to time to Jesuits whose judgement I value, and to a man they told me that it was clearly God's Will for me to stay put.

My mother was at her prayers as usual, down in the church, while I was having my little chat with Father Kieran. I was due to return to the tertianship in the morning. As we walked down to the bus stop I gave her the good news. It took her a little while to take it in and adjust her feelings. Her gratitude and relief were all the greater because some of her friends had told her, 'in strict confidence' that I was going back to Australia in September. They added that I was keeping it a secret from her for the present so as not to upset her.

The whole story, from beginning to end, was false, its only effect being, to cast a shadow over my mother's happiness during that lenten period. She told me afterwards that she could not get the thought out of her mind. The agony was all the more painful because she knew that if I did go back to Australia this time, it would be to a land of no return. Why do people act like this? Why did these 'friends' of my mother not check on the 'facts' before presenting her with a bunch of lies?

When I told her the truth her gratitude to Father Kieran for his humanity in dealing with this situation was very great. I advised her to call again to Gardiner Street tomorrow, after I had gone, and thank him. 'You won't be three minutes talking to him,' I told her, 'when you will feel you had known him all your life'. Father Kieran was not everyone's oyster. The same might be said of Christ Himself. But I could never forget his kindness on this occasion, and, I may add, I had further experience of it in his handling of other personal problems of my own, at a later date. I know, too, that he could be exceedingly severe and could punish offenders to a degree which seemed out of all proportion to the offence. I can only say that, in my case, he never failed to 'make the punishment fit the crime'.

Immediately after tertianship, Father Martin Maher, who was in charge of Retreats, assigned me three in a row to be given to communities of nuns. Before I engaged in the first one I spent a few days in Milltown Park. I met a visiting priest there who had come to make a private retreat. He was anxious to make it well, but he felt a little apprehensive about doing it on his own, without a director. I suggested to the Rector that, if he approved, I would be willing to take it on.

I was given full approval. So this priest and I embarked on the great work and he expressed himself grateful at the close, assuring me he had got much help from the few days alone with God.

On the following Monday I went to Carysfort College, Sisters of Mercy, Dublin, to open my first retreat for Sisters. I was very young and inexperienced and I looked it. While I was having a cup of tea before the opening lecture, the Sister who brought it was obviously curious about me, and feared with good reason that the very important retreat, to one hundred and twenty five nuns, might prove to be more than I could handle. Did I like giving retreats, she wanted to know. Yes, very much. (I had given a few to individuals before contacting that priest at Milltown Park, so I felt my reply was in order.) Sister went on to explain that there would be one hundred and twenty five nuns entering my retreat tonight. 'Fine', I told her. 'I think it is as easy, and perhaps easier even, to have a large audience'. So I escaped from the supper-table without giving myself away!

All this happened shortly after Noah came out of the Ark! I am happy to say that it has been my privilege to give many retreats to Sisters since, in many different Orders. They were responsive and appreciative of my efforts. Their generosity and dedication to the spirit of the Order made me realise that I had much to learn and little to give.

I look back on the experience now with much gratitude to God and to them.

Father Michael Egan was a professor of Mathematics for many years in University College, Dublin. His brethren in the Society of Jesus, and his very many friends outside it, rightly regarded him as a most reliable authority on all things spiritual. He had made a profound study of the two great contemplatives, St. John of the Cross and St. Teresa. He directed many earnest souls in the ways of prayer. He laid immense emphasis on the truth that God is our loving Father and we, as Our Lord taught, His little children. There was nothing harsh or forbidding or frightening or stilted in the direction he gave, but he did insist on the truth that a loving father makes full allowance for the foibles of His small children. He stressed the need of childlikeness in our dealings with our heavenly Father, but he would be no partisan to a humanitarian indulgence in God which one feels, uneasily, may be tending to worm its way into the lives of some of us today.

He created an atmosphere of peace and tranquillity in his social relations with others. This was due to the enviable habit he had acquired of looking on God as a loving Father, and on himself as a devoted son. He took this simply, for granted. He never lost it.

It was enhanced by a delicious sense of humour. Often he gave direction in what he called doggerel verses. Here he proved himself to be a master in the art of coating the pill. It got the truth across. It was accepted and swallowed with a grin. It drew a smile every time the dose was administered, and it was frequently repeated for the amusement it gave to others.

Father Egan frequently wrote these verses for nuns. That is why I am introducing him here in My Last Book, in this section which is reserved exclusively for them. The verses make pleasant reading and I suggest that the pleasure will be increased if they are read aloud. Here is a typical one:

'Dear Sister you are not to fret,
Nor let your conscience be upset,
Because one day you failed to smother
Your feelings towards the Reverend Mother,
But prayed a big big D might seize her
'Cos try your best you couldn't please her.

Of course, dear Sister, it was not right
For you to make a fuss and fight,
About your Sisters and your Ma
Saying that some of them were blisters
And others diplomatic twisters

Don't knock their silly heads together,
Better to talk about the weather.
For stories of domestic strife
Won't help you in your spiritual life.
Nor will your soul grow more interior
Through criticising your Superior.

5 Sorrow

In June, 1947, I think it was, I travelled from Milltown Park to open a retreat that evening in the Convent of Mercy, Doon, Co. Limerick. Early that morning I had discovered my mother, making her way home from Mass, to her little house in Hollybank Avenue. There was fierce rain and a strong and bitter east wind, and, as I write at this moment, I can see her struggling desperately to keep her umbrella open over her head. I caught up with her and helped her home. She sank into an armchair, trying to give the impression when I asked her anxiously, that she was 'fine'.

She revived somewhat after breakfast but I had serious misgivings about leaving her, although I realised very well that she had many kind neighbours on all sides, who loved her and would give her every attention. Still, I was unhappy about going off to Doon under the circumstances and I suggested that I could get a substitute to take over the retreat for me. She would not hear of it. There was no reason for alarm. She really felt quite well. The little set-back she had got was not worth a moment's consideration.

This was characteristic of her. In her eyes, any task I might have to do in my capacity as a priest was something sacred and she would never permit herself to obtrude. So, reluctantly enough, I said goodbye and set out for the train to Limerick.

On the afternoon of the final day of the retreat a telegram arrived telling me I should return as soon as possible. The Sisters at Doon kindly allowed me to advance the hour of the last lecture of the retreat and drove me into Limerick. But Dublin was nearly two hundred miles away, and the last train, and the last bus, and the last plane had all gone. Alfie Sexton, a school companion of mine in St. Munchin's College, came forward to help me. He put his car at my disposal and a driver who would leave me at my mother's halldoor. I never forgot his kindness. Every mile of the road seemed like five, but ultimately we got there. Thanks be to God my mother was at least alive. Kind people had phoned several hospitals during the day, but there was an epidemic in the city and there seemed to be not even one available bed.

I said Mass next morning at the convent of the Sisters of Charity, close by, for whom, then and forever since, I have always had a very sincere regard. I told my sad story to the Sacristan and asked if Mother Bernard Carew, Superior General of the Congregation, was at home. 'Mother General is at home, father, and take it from me that she will find a bed for your mother somewhere.' She did. There was a very heavy snow and the convent telephone was out of order. Mother General made her way down to the local post office and from there managed to get through to St. Vincent's Hospital. She was successful. My dear mother, within a few hours, was comfortably settled in bed. To this day my heart goes out in gratitude to Mother Bernard, and every year, for the rest of her life, I wrote to her on the feast of her Patron, telling her my Mass would be offered for her on that day.

Under the careful nursing at St. Vincent's my mother began to revive. Miss Lillah Murray invited her to come out for a month or two to convalesce at St. Joseph's Guest House, Tivoli Road, Dun Laoghaire. She accepted, and, indeed, she remained there till her death two and a half years later. Nothing could equal the love and care lavished on her by Miss Murray and her community. My mother was very happy there and many times spoke of the Sisters' outstanding charity and otherworldliness.

These Sisters are known as the Daughters of the Immaculate Heart of Mary. They were founded during the French Revolution and for this reason they had always to dress as lay people. St. Pius X said that if they had not been already founded, he would have founded them himself. At present they number about five thousand Sisters, scattered through the five continents. They undertake the care of orphans, they run schools, help priests in parish work, and, generally, they are prepared to undertake any form of apostolate to help the Church and souls.

Miss Murray had immense gifts of mind and heart and she used them exclusively for the service of God and the good of souls. There was in her character a notable proportion between firmness and gentleness. She was Provincial and Superior at

Tivoli Road for many years, during which the activities of the community expanded. As a girl in the world she was teaching in school and, in-between, nursing her invalid mother. She always longed to be a nun, but there seemed no chance as long as her mother needed her. This she had come to accept. Her spiritual director at this time was the Jesuit, Father Francis Browne. She explained her position to him one day. His reply astonished her and filled her with joy. 'Child', he said. 'It is quite possible for you to become a nun and continue living at home and looking after your mother at the same time'. This possibility had never remotely occurred to her. She found her way into the convent in Tivoli Road and lived for a long time in the Society, combining in a remarkable way, a life of almost incessant activity, with a close and intimate union with Christ in continual prayer.

In point of fact I got back here to Gardiner Street only recently, after spending two weeks at St. Joseph's. It is a breath of fresh air to go there from time to time and see at close range how that spirit is flourishing still. There are four very promising novices. A spirit of love and joy permeates the whole atmosphere. The gentleness and firmness bequeathed to the community live on still. I think that any girl who may be fostering the idea of entering religious life might be advised to visit St. Joseph's. She would be encouraged and advised but without undue pressure.

In 1949 I was giving another retreat, this time at Milltown Park, to a group of about fifty Jesuits, priests, brothers and students. Some of the students were due for ordination at the end of the retreat. About halfway through, another urgent message came, this time from St. Joseph's, Tivoli Road, and this was to be the final call. They sent it unknown to my mother, fearing she might object to disturbing the retreat. Father O'Grady, the Rector, was almost as distressed as I was myself. I offered to carry on with the retreat and keep in touch with St. Joseph's by phone. He wouldn't hear of this. I was to forget about the retreat. He packed me straightaway into a taxi and instructed the driver to put me down at Tivoli Road.

With a stab at my heart I realised, after the first glance, that this was the end. My mother tried to smile a little, she raised her hand and took hold of mine and whispered: 'I think He's coming for me this time'. She was right. We prayed all the time. I gave her a last absolution, secretly wondering if there was anything to absolve. Characteristically one of the Sisters brought me a cup of tea and a biscuit on a plate. I demurred. 'Take it,' my mother told me. 'It is God's gift'. In less than an hour she was gone.

I prefer not to describe my reactions, beyond saying that I was stunned and suddenly isolated from all I held dear. I was alone in an empty world. I went to where she would have me go, down to the chapel to pray for strength and unreserved acceptance. For days I went about dazed, feeling that I would never give another mission or retreat, only numbed and insensible. It was like a nightmare.

When writing to another priest later on, to sympathise with him on the death of his mother, I told him he could thank God because he had put over him the heaviest cross he would ever have to carry. To another, the best friend I have, whose position was very like my own, I said: 'I don't want to rub it in with salt, but the day your mother dies you will shed tears of blood.' He reminded me of this when the Lord did actually come and take her to Himself. I saw reproduced in him exactly what had happened in my own case. Messages of sympathy and promises of Masses poured in from all sides, and they did much to ease the pain.

After I had been living in this state of stupor for perhaps two weeks my Uncle Joe came to speak with me. He took me aside and warned me very seriously that my mother would want no more of this. I must pull myself together. There was plenty of good work waiting for me to do. The prayers of so many good friends would get me the grace I needed. They did. Thanks be to God.

My mother had died on 27 July 1949.

6 Problems and Changes

It is now some sixty years since Father Gerald Fitzgerald founded an Order of Priests and Brothers whose mission it would be to help in every possible way problem priests. He was a very happy man when a letter came to him from Rome giving him full permission and a blessing. Pope John XXIII wrote to him:

> Our paternal heart was greatly consoled, beloved son, when We learned of your very commendable apostolate among the Lord's anointed, who, while bearing the heat of the day and the burden, have fallen a prey to the insidious snares of evil that beset the path of priests. Your work on their behalf is like that of the Good Samaritan, for you heal their wounds, nursing them lovingly back to spiritual health and clothing them again with the radiant vesture of sacerdotal fervour and grace .. If they have been wounded in the fray it is our duty to help them, for they are our brothers, our sick brothers . . .

If Father Fitzgerald knew you were coming he would be at the door waiting to receive you. It was a privilege and a joy for me that he took me to his heart and invited me to give retreats to the members of his Order and to the guest-priests. The guests cook and serve the meals. They sweep the floors, look after the gardens, and all the year round provide fruit and potatoes for the table, and flowers and plants for the altars and dining-rooms. 'You could not find a better spirit of charity anywhere in the world,' a visitor remarked. 'The reason,' Father Fitzgerald would explain, 'is that in *Via Coeli*, – the name of the House – there is no pride.'

This spirit of peace and harmony must be traced, before all else, to the care with which supernatural means are employed. Guest priests are asked to spend, every day, a full continuous hour before the Blessed Sacrament and to consecrate themselves to the Immaculate Heart of Mary. Human nature being what it is we are not surprised that there is an occasional blow-up, but generally it proves to be a storm in a tea-cup. Sometimes a guest will pack up and go off in a temper, but invariably he will cool down and return, and the Paracletes are the first to understand and the incident is soon forgotten.

As I was writing this chapter it occurred to me that I had been out of touch with these men for a considerable period. I wondered how the Order and its apostolate had been faring so I wrote to the priest in charge of 'Foundation House,' to find out. [His name and address are: Father Busca, Jemez Springs, Servants of the Holy Paraclete, New Mexico 87025. The Order has also a House at: Our Lady of Victory, North Strand, Browneshill, Gloucester, England. Phone: Brinscomb 3084.]

It was most consoling to hear from Father Busca that the work has developed by leaps and bounds, almost miraculously. I wish I could incorporate his entire letter. The following will at least give some inkling as to the vast developments which have taken place over the years.

> In the early days we depended mostly on the power of prayer to help the priests who came to us with their problems. However we soon came to realise that grace builds on nature. We had to admit that we were not properly trained in the various disciplines to be really effective. So, according to the talents given to each of us by God, we began to train systematically in the fields of spirituality, spiritual direction, prayer, sexuality, psychiatry, etc. We have had to regroup our members and set up various centres to co-ordinate our apostolate.

The members of the Order are officially known as: The Servants of the Holy Paraclete. The needs of their guests must always be their primary concern; their own rôle is to be quite literally, their servants, waiting on them, even as Christ Himself became the servant of us all. It is an ideal at once ennobling and demanding. Who can join the Order permanently? 'Priests who have experienced a distinct attraction for helping their brother-priests and who have the full permission of their bishop or religious superior, may qualify to test their vocation in the novitiate.' A Jesuit was so favourably impressed by all he saw, that, after much serious prayer and deliberation, he asked to be dispensed from his Jesuit vows and become a servant of the Holy Paraclete. At 85 he is still hale and hearty, a dedicated priest and a highly-skilled mechanic to boot, with a genius for thinking out schemes for the benefit of the Order.

Another priest writes: 'Every night I kneel before the Blessed Sacrament and thank Jesus and Mary for bringing me here. As a young priest when outside, I was supposed to be a good preacher and I was being constantly invited to take the pulpit on special occasions. That gift could easily have puffed me up with pride and led me to disaster. But there is no pride here, thank God.'

I recall a long talk I had with one of the Servants. Among other things, he told me that he had come across an unfortunate man – I forget how – whom he suspected of being a priest. The poor man was living in a hovel, in rags, grimy, unwashed and unshaved. He resented bitterly the efforts of the Servant to pry into his affairs. But ultimately the grace of God triumphed. He came to the House, was washed and shaved and dressed in a brand-new clerical suit. But, best of all, he was brought back to the priesthood, living for eleven years with the Servants, during every day of which he celebrated Mass and recited his Office. 'If the whole Order did nothing more than this,' I said, 'it would have justified its existence a hundred times over. Is that priest buried in your cemetery outside, father?' 'Yes.' 'I'm going out right now to kneel at his grave and pray, *for* him and *to* him.' 'Fine. And pray also in the same way for the priest buried beside him, on his right hand, whose story is very similar to his.'

> As a human person the priest needs to be recognised and appreciates the warmth of being loved. Like any other human being the priest wants to be accepted. He wants to belong, to be and to feel needed. He, like other people, passes through various discernible stages in life's growth. He has the need for some recognition of his efforts and respect for his person. Like others he searches for intimacy with his God and struggles to integrate his life in the presence of his Lord.

A year or two ago I was sitting alone in a railway carriage. A young priest looked in from the corridor, saw the empty carriage and smilingly indicated that he would like to join me. Of course.

We got talking, I forget how, about clerical dress. He was complete with black clothes, Roman collar 'and all'. He did not always wear it he told me, and, indeed, he thought too much importance was sometimes attached to it. I agreed, up to a point. This young priest, a Jesuit like myself, might be able to enlighten me. There could be no doubt about the mind and wish of the Holy Father in the matter. Three or four times he strongly recommended, almost ordered, that priests and nuns and religious, should dress in the manner befitting their profession. I told my friend that, unless all I had ever learned during my years in the Society about obedience was wrong, I could see no justification for refusing to obey such a definite expression of the Pope's wishes.

I know many excellent priests who travel about regularly in lay clothes. I don't condemn them, but I would be interested to know how they get around what the Pope has so strongly and so repeatedly recommended. It seemed to me that he had gone as far as he could short of giving a direct command. I remembered that St. Ignatius was something of an innovator in not prescribing 'any fixed habit' for his men. But he was at least equally emphatic in insisting on unqualified and absolute obedience to every indication of *any* superior's will, and surely this would include the Sovereign Pontiff. It is a considerable time since the Pope has expressed his will in this matter. He has told us what to do and he does not want to make an issue of it. If a priest or a religious fails in this matter I cannot see how he or she can claim to be absolutely loyal and still disregard so clear an indication of the Pope's wishes.

I assured my fellow-traveller that I said all this in no spirit of harsh criticism. I was genuinely puzzled. I was looking for the answer. That was all. Reluctantly I have to confess that I got no nearer to the answer that day. My companion talked a fair bit round about the point, but I felt that at the end he left me back at square one.

Since our interview the following paragraphs have been published in the Press.

> Pope John Paul II has ordered all priests living in Rome to shun wearing civilian clothes and wear their clerical garb, 'to demonstrate the sacred character of their priestly mission'. The Vatican announced this yesterday. The Pontiff, who has often stressed the need for priests to dress in clerical garb, gave this instruction in a letter to the Pope's Vicar in Rome, Cardinal Ugo Poletti.
>
> Explaining why the order was addressed only to the diocese of Rome and not the entire Church, Cardinal Poletti said the Pope would like 'the sons and brothers' in the city, to set an example

> for all others to follow. He said the order also applied to all members of Religious Orders, as well as to foreign and Italian clergymen living in or visiting Rome.
>
> One Vatican source said the Pontiff despite his remarkable appeals, was dismayed to see some priests at pastoral functions wearing casual slacks and sweaters, with only a cross pinned on their lapels.
>
> Earlier, at Maynooth, the Holy Father had said to priests, diocesan and religious, and to students: 'To you students and to you priests, diocesan and regular, I say: Rejoice to be witnesses to Christ in the modern world. Do not hesitate to be recognisable, identifiable, in the streets as men and women who have consecrated their lives to God and who have given up everything worldly to follow Christ. Believe in the value for contemporary men and women of the visible signs of your consecrated lives. People need signs and reminders of God in the modern secular city, which has few reminders of God left. Do not help the trend towards "taking God off the streets" by adopting secular modes of dress and behaviour. . . .'

We went on from there, my young friend and I, to the matter of wearing vestments when saying Mass. He generally wore them, but he inclined to the view that their use should be optional. I referred him back to the Old Testament and to the extraordinary care shown by the Lord in prescribing the use of vestments and to His insistence on every minute detail. If the Lord was so concerned about vestments in the Old Law, which after all was only a prelude to the perfect sacrifice of the New, surely it was fair to argue that He would have been much more insistent when prescribing vestments when there was question of the holy sacrifice of the Mass. Again I was only seeking light in a genuine difficulty, and again I fear my friend left me where he found me.

We had some words about concelebrated Masses. He told me he sometimes had concelebrated with fifty or sixty other priests. I have seen such Masses, and the sight is undoubtedly most moving, and emphasizes, as it is meant to do, the brotherhood of all us priests one with another and with Christ. But this old priest thanked God when he read in the Council Documents that priests were always perfectly free to celebrate alone or with a group. I find it difficult to concentrate on what I am doing, to keep 'in step' with the other concelebrants. Since Vatican II, I think I cannot have concelebrated more than ten or twelve times in all.

Had there been more time I think we might have found something to say about devotion to the Holy Spirit and the Charismatics. I have often been asked what I thought of them – not that that is matter of any great consequence. My answer is that these prayer-groups have been blessed and approved in many parts of the world by the competent Church authorities, that many excellent Catholics have explained to me, with great joy, that their understanding of prayer and the consolation it brings and the courage to bear the crosses of life, have all marvellously developed as a result of this sharing in prayer. I have been at some meetings of this sort – one I recall in particular – where the fervour and sincerity of the participants was most affecting.

But, before venturing on a definite opinion, I prefer to await an authoritative statement from the Church. I'd like to quote St. John, for myself and others. 'Dearly beloved', he writes, 'believe not every spirit, but try the spirits if they be of God, because many false prophets are gone out into this world'.

I find help too in the story about Gameliel in the fifth chapter of the Acts of the Apostles. He was a Pharisee, a doctor of the Law, respected by all the people. The Jews, infuriated by the numbers embracing Christianity, were debating how to handle the situation. Gameliel stood up and told them to 'take heed what you intend to do with these men . . . Let them alone, for if this council or work be of men it will be brought to nothing. But if it be of God you cannot overthrow it'. It seems to me that to quote this sound advice for anyone asking what to think about the Charismatics is to give them a most reasonable standpoint.

It is a truism to say that in the past fifty or sixty years there have been vast changes in the Church and in the world. In my early Jesuit life my contemporaries and I thought we had all the answers. Oldsters we regarded with a certain amount of intolerance, because they could not be made to see our point of view in many matters, and persisted in walking out of step with us who were conscious of the pressing need of change. Evidence of this attitude I see today too. When asked: 'What do you think of all the changes?' I used, at first, to express deep sorrow for many of them and feel an anxiety lest we be sweeping under the carpet part of our precious

Ignatian treasures. Specific instances cited did nothing to restore my peace of mind.

I am still somewhat unhappy with some of the changes. But in many cases too, I have come to recognise their necessity and the advantages they bring in the present state of the Church and the world. In this I have found much help and guidance in the teaching of Vatican II, though some cynics might maintain that it is an umbrella wide enough to include a conglomeration of theories weird and difficult to accept.

In a letter to Father Arrupe I once told him I was coming around to making my own Our Lord's direction to St. Peter. Peter asked Christ what was going to happen to St. John. He got the somewhat terse reply: 'What has that to do with you? You follow Me'. Father Arrupe thought the cap fitted me perfectly. I have been wearing it ever since and enjoying much peace of soul.

I learned that any complaint or censure I made during the days of my schooling did not have the slightest effect in bringing about any change. I saw the exact same result in the case of some of my colleagues. They waxed eloquent on the dangers and abuses; they were listened to. They waited to see what practical effect their suggestions might produce only to find that all their eloquence had spent itself on the desert air.

I once relayed for Father Thomas Byrne, when he was Provincial, some bitter complaints made to me by another Jesuit. He asked me if I had known Father Michael Browne. I had, of course. And Father John Sullivan? Yes. What did I think of them? 'Two saints', I answered. And did I think they did not see material for harsh criticism? Of course they did. Did I ever hear a word of complaint? Never, I had to admit. So my Father Provincial left it to me to take the lesson home. I have made some considerable advance in that direction, I think. 'What has that to do with you? You follow Me'.

Young priests this old man finds, by and large, to be most courteous and anxious to help. An engaged couple, Cathal and Agnes O'Doherty came to me to ask if I would say the Mass and join them in holy matrimony on their great day. I very gladly consented. But as the arrangements developed I began to have some misgivings. In all my years as a priest I don't suppose I 'did' more than six or seven marriages. Some days before this one, on studying the document, I found myself almost completely at sea. The whole ritual seemed so involved, with so many pages to be turned back and forward, that, in all honesty, I was seriously worried. In my distress I turned to a young priest who was thoroughly acquainted with all that had to be done.

He was wonderful. He signed all the papers in advance, showed me everything in the documents, and went off satisfied that I would have no further difficulty. I stumbled through, somehow, and hoped for the best. When all was over I consoled myself with the thought that it was the two spouses who had administered the sacrament to each other, not the priest. So, in my case, the marriage was, at least, valid!

But of this I am quite certain: If I live for another fifty years as a priest I'll never do another!

Before going on, I would like to give two quotations, exemplifying different attitudes towards the changes in the Church. The first quotation is from Malcolm Muggeridge. In his book on Mother Teresa *Something Beautiful for God*, he has the following passage:

> Today the Church, for inscrutable reasons of its own, has decided to have a reformation, just when the previous one, Luther's, is finally running into the sand. I make no judgement about something which, as a non-member, is no concern of mine. But *if* I were a member I should be forced to say that, in my opinion, if men were to be stationed at the doors of Churches, with whips to drive worshippers away, or inside the Religious Orders specifically to discourage vocations, or among the clergy to spread alarm and despondency, they could not hope to be more effective in achieving those ends, than are the trends and policies seemingly now dominant within the Church.

The writer of this passage and his wife have since been received into the Catholic Church.

Our second quotation, from four centuries ago, is the calm assurance and sound advice of St. John of the Cross.

> See that thou become not of a sudden sorrowful because of the adversities that are in the world, since thou knowest not the blessings that they bring with them, being ordained in the judgement of God for the everlasting joy of the elect.

An age like ours, from every analogy in history, should be prolific in saints.

In *The Furrow*, for September, 1982, Father Frank Sammon, S.J., has an article on the changing Church. He calls it: *Towards a New Image of Church and Society*. The Church in recent years has gone through a series of revolutionary changes in thinking about itself. . . . We can say that it has been turned upside-down, inside-out, and back-to-front. *Upside down*, because today the stress is laid on the fact that all Christians participate in the Church, whereas heretofore the emphasis was put on the salvation given to individuals who maintain their membership of the Church.

Inside out means that the Church no longer devotes itself in an exclusive way to its own members and its own structures. It stresses the very consoling text from St. Paul that 'God *wants all men* to be saved'. Certainly the Church is central to God's plan of salvation, but the link between salvation and the Church had to be thought out in a better way.

Back to Front. This means that instead of being over-solicitous about preserving all our past traditions . . . on the whole looking to the future and how it should be shaped in a more human way has been taking place.

Father Sammon develops these three thoughts in a way that is intriguing and reassuring on the whole, though one might hesitate before accepting it in its entirety.

Sometimes when I hear men of my generation talking about the past one might imagine that we were all perfect then, that our observance left nothing to be desired, that obedience, in letter and spirit – so prized by St. Ignatius – was always prompt and willing and accepted unquestioningly when it tested some of us severely. To this I want to say, bluntly and truthfully, that we had many shortcomings and sometimes they were glaring enough. There was much insistence on external observance of rules, and, as I note elsewhere, a harshness in dealing with offenders which could have produced in them a spirit of inward defiance and even rebellion. St. Francis de Sales' teaching would have obviated this, to the effect that 'you will catch more flies with a spoonful of honey than with a barrel of vinegar.'

I see much for which to thank God in the spirit which has developed since Vatican II. Looking back on the past with St. Paul he might have told us: 'I gave you milk to drink, not meat, for you were not able as yet'. Much more freedom is given us today and the change is a welcome one and it is proper. But no system is without its dangers and danger there is that all, or nearly all, external observance is flung out the window. Father Diarmuid Dubay has written a book called: *Can Religious Life Survive?* It is published by Veritas. It takes a very balanced, objective view of our present position in religious life.

His final conclusion is: 'Yes, Religious life will survive, because there will always be generous souls who want to live a life of complete consecration to God. But if you ask me: Will it survive in this or that specific Congregation, I'm not at all so sure'.

I once repeated for a youngish priest what I heard as a small boy, dinned into our ears, night after night at a parish mission. After the rosary the priest would say: 'When you lie down to sleep at night, fold your arms in the form of a cross and repeat slowly: "I must die. I do not know when, nor how, nor where. But this I know – that if I die in mortal sin I am lost forever. Jesus have mercy on me and grant me the grace of a holy and a happy death."' I told my friend that I doubt if in my long life I ever once omitted this practice.

But he clapped both hands to his head and a look of horror came into his face. If I was sure that he was just 'putting on an act' for the occasion, I would not worry. But he was dead serious. I have to say that this baffles me. What the missioner said is simply a development of the scriptural injunction: 'In all things remember your last end and you will never sin'. Is hell a fact or a myth? It may be a very unpleasant fact, like a cancer, but that is more reason for making sure to avoid it.

Here is a story, for the truth of which I can vouch. A man was sentenced to death for a grievous crime. He sat in his prison cell the evening before, sullen, silent, defiant, stooped. He would have nothing to do with any priest. He refused to repent for what so many knew of his sinful life. Three or four priests tried and got nowhere. A nun came along and she got nowhere. When she was on the point of leaving, she paused and looked at him with pity, sitting over there on his bed, with his head between his hands. 'Tom', she said, 'just think of this – what would not a soul in hell give for five minutes of the chance you are getting?' She was gone, but the penny dropped. Poor Tom turned to God, made a good confession, received Holy Communion and the sacrament of the sick. He prayed all night. Next morning the priest walked with him to his death.

Of course we are to serve God from the motive of love. Of course we depend on His mercy. But is an old priest justified in fearing that the tendency to bypass the truth of sin and of hell is to play straight into the devil's hands?

I am no pessimist. I repeat that from every analogy in history an age like ours should be prolific in saints. Ours is no exception. It is, rather, an inspiring confirmation of that truth. Father Bolland, readers will perhaps remember, was the priest in charge of us during tertianship, the year following theology.

I find myself often recalling the earnestness of the instructions, spiced with his delicious sense of Scottish dry humour. He told us one day to be 'afraid of an easy life'. The cult of softness was invading the world and nothing would be easier than to adopt its principles, even in our Jesuit life. 'Unless a man renounce himself he cannot be My disciple'. That sentence stands firm.

I repeated this to a Jesuit who is very much 'with it' in his attitude towards life. No sooner were the words 'be afraid of an easy life' out of my mouth than he got very excited and nearly jumped on me! 'Not at all! You must be yourself, bound to live your own life. All that self-conquest stuff is out since Vatican II.'

Poor Vatican II, how many crimes are committed in your name! Be yourself? I had always the impression that St. Ignatius insisted firmly on conquering self. This appears in the very title of his Exercises; 'Certain Spiritual Exercises whereby a man learns to *conquer himself* so as to come to a decision without being biased by any inordinate affection'. That goes right through Ignatian spirituality. To throw it out the window is to throw out the baby with the bath-water.

It is one thing not to like self-conquest and to feel ashamed at having to admit how small a place it may have in one's actual life. But it is ruinous to substitute 'be yourself' for it. If that be advocated and put into practice what becomes of the demanding sentence from the lips of Christ? 'If any man will come after Me, let him deny himself, take up his cross daily and follow Me?'.

7 Going Places

> Two men went over the mountain, and what do you think they saw? The other side of the mountain, so what do you think they did? They climbed back over the mountain and told us all they saw.

The late Father Brendan Barry, during the absence of our Father Provincial, was appointed as his substitute. I phoned him one day and explained that I was going to France on retreat work, and I wondered if he would be kind enough to allow me climb over the mountain dividing France and Spain and see the other side. 'Why not?' I thanked him sincerely but I hurried to hang up fearing he might change his mind. He didn't. What happened as a result has such happy and interesting memories for me that I cannot refrain from calling some of them to mind and giving them a few pages in my last book.

Spain, land teeming with history; covered with monuments which fascinated you as they unfolded their stories stretching way back into the centuries; Spain, with its long history of loyalty to the Church and its long list of canonised saints – all this and much more made the other side of the mountain a land quivering with interest.

And what do you think we saw? It would be an impertinence to dogmatize about problems and the solutions offered and I have carefully side-stepped that danger. I regard myself, rather, as a Press correspondent, putting on record just what I have seen and heard.

Mary told me that Avila is about the size of Thomastown, and Mary, who is a much-travelled person, has been, not only to Avila but to Thomastown as well. So she knows. During one of her visits to Avila she was conducted through a portion of the Carmelite Church, where tradition says St. Teresa was born four hundred years ago. The friar who showed her around unlocked the door of that very room and bade her enter. Inside, she saw a man kneeling motionless in prayer. His eyes were closed, his face pale and emaciated. He took not the slightest notice of the two visitors, absorbed as he was in his devotions. On coming out, the priest locked the door again, leaving him behind – but not alone.

He was Allison Peers, brilliant student of Carmelite spirituality, who has written profusely about it, and given to the world a masterly and critical translation of all the works of St. John of the Cross and St. Teresa. He loved to spend whole hours in this spot hallowed by so many memories of the saint. He would plunge his soul into prayer. He would drink deep draughts of the fountains of the Saviour. He would taste and see for himself and experience for himself what he tries to put into words. A marvellous intimacy developed between this man and his God. Allison Peers never became a Catholic. Father Paul O'Dea, mentioned elsewhere, used to say that if he had been a Catholic he would almost certainly have been canonised.

The nuns in Madrid had written in advance to a Spanish priest in Avila, Don Gregorio, telling him to take me under his wing. Nothing could exceed his kindness and courtesy. He was quite determined that I should miss none of the treasures which Avila has to show. I felt like Tobias in the Old Testament who was guided throughout a long and difficult journey by Raphael, an archangel in disguise. I named Don Gregorio, Raphael, and Robert Nash, Tobias.

Before he could stretch out his hand to greet me, he had first to unwind himself from the folds of an enormous cloak which enveloped him completely, revealing nothing but a head protruding from the top. That cloak was to intrigue me. On investing himself he would take one flap in his right hand and throw it as far as it could go over his left shoulder, the result being that he reminded one for all the world of a Roman senator complete with his toga.

We sat down and began to discuss plans. I drew from my breast pocket a bulky envelope and handed it to him. His eyes sparkled with delight as he read. On the previous evening I had sought and had been granted an audience with the Apostolic Nuncio in Madrid. I explained to him that I was an Irish Jesuit, that I sometimes did some writing, that I hoped to put on paper some of my experiences for my people when I returned to Ireland. On this account I had taken my courage in my hands to seek this interview with His Excellency to place a petition before him. Would he authorise me to go, with another priest, into the enclosure of both the Carmelite convents in Avila? He said yes, most graciously, adding that he would leave a written document at his office stating this. It would be waiting there for me early in the morning. I thanked him profusely, and, as when I was dealing with Father Brendan Barry, I got away as soon as possible before His Excellency would have time to change his mind!

That document Don Gregorio was now holding, his eyes sparkling. He had been here in Avila for more than thirty years and had never once this privilege in all that time. He was as excited as an actor, about to step out of the wings and on to the stage to take a major rôle. We would go together in the morning to the Incarnation Carmel, and to St. Joseph's Carmel on the morning following.

The Incarnation Convent is about a mile outside the city. We walked in the very footsteps of St. Teresa, when she set out on that day four hundred years ago, all on her own, to beg to be admitted as a novice. Her father loved her dearly and refused to let her go. So she took the law into her own hands and just ran away from home.

It cost her much anguish. Later she would state that she suffered such poignant sorrow on that day that she believed the pains of death could not equal it.

The community then numbered about one hundred and thirty nuns. They followed a rule which had become mitigated. The mitigations were condoned; those who should have corrected them turned a blind eye. There were prolonged visits and feastings, shared with the secular friends and relatives outside. The nuns, for the most part, fed their minds on the scraps of news and gossip which seeped in from outside. These divided the mind and the heart between them and God, these trivialities getting the larger share. Distractions multiplied and prayer degenerated into a wearisome burden, a sort of nightmare to be cast off at the first specious excuse.

Later in life Teresa issued most solemn warnings against entering a Religious Order in which the Rule had become seriously relaxed. She would much prefer the prospective novice to remain 'in the world'. Parents must not delude themselves into thinking that because a daughter of theirs had entered a convent, she was thereby rendered immune from all spiritual danger.

But there is no laxity in the Incarnation Convent today. I said Mass there on that morning, being privileged to use the chalice used by St. John of the Cross. After the Mass, the ancient door, which had opened to admit St. Teresa four hundred years ago, swung back on its hinges. We were back straightaway into the sixteenth century. The nuns could talk about nothing only 'Holy Mother'. Here is the stairs on top of which she saw the infant Jesus standing, while she knelt on the lowest step. All the scenes of her life are faithfully depicted here, the room where she used to sit on the floor, her pen flying rapidly and covering page after page of her wondrous books. Here is the room where her heart was pierced by a dart thrust into it by the hand of an angel. 'I saw him', she wrote, 'with a long dart of gold in his hand and it seemed to me that at the top there was fire . . . I remained all aflame with a great love of God . . . The discourse between God and the soul is so sweet that I crave Him in His goodness to give a taste of it to him who might think I am lying. . . .'

I confess, as I write about Teresa of Avila, that some readers might think the contemplative life irrelevant today. This would be a fatal error. We cannot all enter contemplative monasteries, but we all need the contemplative spirit if our exterior efforts to bring souls to Christ are to meet with the success they deserve. All external apostleship, to be truly effective, must be the overflowing of the prayer of the apostle.

Since I wrote this Pope John Paul II visited this convent. I saw a picture of him surrounded by the community. It needed no effort to believe that there was a flutter in the dovecot. Delight shone in every face. I imagine they must still be talking about this unprecedented event.

I very much wish to say something about a place called Bozo del Tio Rainmundo and its dedicated apostle, Father Llanos, one of two Jesuits working there. I travelled to the place in a somewhat over-crowded bus. When I intimated that I was anxious to meet this priest, a chorus of voices began, and a nodding of heads clearly expressed that he was well known to them all, that they loved and admired him.

I found him sitting in a rickety chair in front of a typewriter. The room was chilly and unheated. He had a small bed in the corner, another chair like the one he was using, a picture or two and a crucifix, and books galore. He is a prolific writer and his Provincial allows him to contribute the royalties on his books towards the up-keep of his immense parish.

My first impression was that there was a poor man who had undertaken more than he could cope with. He seemed depressed by his experiences and said he was surprised that I should travel all this distance merely to see his poverty-stricken parish. His face was serious. I don't think he smiled once, even when greeting me.

There is certainly nothing glamorous about his mission. The poor people are illiterate, uncouth in manner if judged by the standards to which he had been accustomed. They appreciate what he is trying to do for them. He hopes and prays that, little by little, spiritual truths will appeal more strongly to them. What he is attempting to do is only the beginning of a gigantic task, calling for many more priests and nuns, teachers and nurses.

He has some 22,000 in his parish. All are baptised; nearly all are married in the Church; few pass out of this world without receiving the sacraments. If you ask any of them, men, women or children, what their religion is, you will be told with emphasis that they are all Catholics. But their concept of what being a Catholic means is infantile. There are five Masses every Sunday, and, out of the 22,000 parishioners, some 2,000 attend, most of them women and children. He has no illusions, and I could not but feel that the going was hard.

The very wealthy, who could give a lot of help, for the most part are not interested. They prefer to contribute to charities which are more spectacular. He has organised a sale of bottles on a large scale. This brings in a fair amount. He was not complaining, only giving answer to my questions according as I asked them. He has put up a chapel, schools, and a workshop. With his fellow-Jesuit, four nuns, and a staff of lay teachers, the children receive the best education possible for them under the circumstances. The girls learn knitting, cooking, cushion-making, sewing. The boys are taught carpentry, carving, how to make and repair boots and shoes.

As far as he can, Father Llanos supplies the materials in all cases. There is no charge and all profits go to the producer. This arrangement, of course, stimulates industry and initiative and there are gratifying results.

Would I like to see around the place? He brought me first to the chapel where the Blessed Sacrament is reserved and where he says Mass every morning. A plain wooden altar and a crucific are the work of some of his apprentices. On the walls he has the eight beatitudes, to try to teach his poor people the blessings reserved for those who learn the hard lesson of patience in enduring. Off the chapel is a hall where he puts on a dance on Sunday nights and an occasional show. Some patron presented him with a television set.

He brought me to the crêche where there must have been at least a hundred tiny infants. The mothers were all out at work, and he employs nurses to take care of the children till they return each evening. He has made out a list of persons who are sick or unable to find work. To these he supplies, *gratis*, to the best of his power, the food and nourishment they require.

One little lad of four and a half appeared on the scene, sent by his mother to collect food. He opened out his big canvas bag and got what he wanted. Frequently as he went the rounds, Father Llanos was held up. His people bring him their problems, ask questions, and he helps to settle their disputes. He showed me over the different shops and factories and introduced me to the boys and girls being taught there. He has many promising youngsters. He has established the Sodality of Our Lady and prays it may flourish. His four nuns and his Jesuit colleague are with him, heart and soul, in his noble efforts.

I thought he was more cheerful now, so I ventured to emphasise, not the good which was still waiting to be done but rather the solid achievement already secured. Because he was here, all those mothers could go out to work with minds at rest about their babies. Because he was here more than two thousand people were going to Mass on Sundays, who would miss it otherwise. Because he was here these hundreds of boys and girls were being fitted for a useful and purposeful life in the future. And, apart from any visible results, there was his own generous offer of himself for this work, in so many ways thankless. It is some years since I met him, but his noble example has remained with me all the time, as a stimulus and a challenge.

On my return journey to Madrid I sat in my upholstered cushion for about a quarter of an hour before anything began to happen. Apparently the system was that the driver waits till he has a full complement of passengers. They drifted in and sat and chatted. There was no fixed time for starting! One young man intimated that he knew exactly where I wanted to go. Father Llanos had told him, and he would keep me on the straight and narrow.

One of our party, a boy of ten or eleven, followed me after I had left the bus to make sure I would find the underground. I thanked him and offered him a few coins. Did I intend this money for him to buy my ticket for me? I said no, of course, and I pointed to his pocket to indicate that it was for himself. From a poor little lad it came as an especially gracious act. My other guide insisted on accompanying me to the very door of the shop I was looking for, and only with great difficulty could I prevail on him to accept a tiny gift in return for his kindness.

More recent information makes pleasant reading. It would seem to justify a well-founded optimism for the future of the Church and its relations with the workman in this great Catholic land.

Father Llanos and I corresponded for quite a time after my return to Ireland, and, through the generosity of some of my friends I was in the happy position to be able to send him a little financial help.

Jesus was born in the cave at Bethlehem. The Society which has the honour to bear His name was born in a cave at Manresa. For nearly a year Ignatius fasted severely and inflicted voluntary penance on himself in Manresa. But this was secondary. The outstanding fact about Manresa is that there the saint attained such a close union with God in prayer, and there he set down his Spiritual Exercises, by the correct and persevering use of which we too can hope to follow him and reach out to a state when prayer would become habitual with us.

To my sorrow I did not get to Manresa during my visit. But I have no difficulty in visualising him there, kneeling in the semi-darkness, directly under the action of the Holy Spirit fashioning his soul to sanctity. Concerning himself he has this to say: 'Life would be for me an intolerable burden if I thought that for a moment there was anything in me which was not wholly subject to Him'.

Before I left Ireland a friend of mine told me, when in Pamplona, to make sure to contact Miss Huarte there. She spoke English and she would be sure to help me in many ways. She lived near the Redemptorist Church in the city. It was a difficult task. Looking for somebody named 'Huarte' in Pamplona is like looking for someone named Paddy Murphy in Cork. But ultimately, through the good offices of one of the Redemptorists, we found her, a splendid Catholic, only too happy to bring me around and show me everything.

The basilica marks the spot where tradition says Ignatius fell when defending the fort here against the attack by the French. There is a fine statue outside the Church, an exact replica of the one in Loyola, showing the saint lying wounded, supported by two soldiers, obviously in great pain and making preparations for his toilsome journey home. The French treated him with the utmost respect, having witnessed his courage, and they gave him every care possible in the circumstances.

The church containing the basilica is now in the care of the Redemptorists. It came into their possession after the Society of Jesus was suppressed in 1773 and it never reverted to the Jesuits. This is no reflection on the Redemptorists. I am told that they offered to restore it but for some reason the negotiations broke down. They welcome every Jesuit who comes along and readily make all arrangements for him to say Mass at the altar of St. Ignatius. I had that privilege and at my Mass I gave Holy Communion to Miss Huarte.

The name of Ignatius, or Inigo, first figures in connection with Pamplona in 1515. These were his wild days, before his conversion, and he fell foul of the law during the carnival celebrations up at Azpeitia. On the plea that he was a cleric – the arguments for this claim cannot be given here – the young man sought asylum and sanctuary in the bishop's prison here in Pamplona.

Fulminations and threats and demands poured into the bishop's residence from Azpeitia, but Inigo, safely lodged, refused to budge, and His Lordship, who himself was also 'agin the Government', was in no hurry to hand over the culprit. Twenty years later Ignatius returned to Azpeitia as a priest and made no secret of the fact that one reason for doing so was to repair the scandal he had given as a young man about town.

Somewhere about 1515 he was prominent in a street brawl here in Pamplona. A group of fellows deliberately collided with him in the street and threw him violently against the wall. Inigo's eyes blazed with fury. He drew his sword and they raced away in terror. Somebody leaped on the shoulders of the enraged Inigo who was in hot pursuit, pinned his arms firmly and refused to let him go till the culprits were well away at a safe distance. There seems to be little doubt that he would have killed some of them, to avenge the slight insult, had he not thus been forcibly restrained. So the tales about Ignatius and Pamplona are not all edifying.

Saints, to borrow Father Broderick's phrase, have 'plenty of red blood in their veins'. And Rene Bazin reminds us that 'saints, like all masterpieces, are slowly made'. It seemed to me worthwhile including this tale as illustrating the tough clay and the pride and the lack of self-control and the vindictiveness with which Ignatius had to grapple and the complete victory he attained in the struggle.

Two complementary texts would have helped him. Christ would have taught him that 'without Me, you can do nothing'. But St. Paul would have added: 'I can do all things in Him Who strengthens me'. To a soul in many ways kindred to Ignatius He spoke these words, full of encouragement: 'Behold how weak thou art. Behold how strong thou art. In thee is all thy weakness. In Me is all thy strength. And, as I am infinitely greater than thou art, therefore is thy strength infinitely greater than thy weakness. And it is I who say to thee: "Arise and walk"'.

Xavier Castle lies as far north of Pamplona as Loyola lies south, about fifty miles, roughly an hour's run in a car. St. Francis Xavier was born here four hundred years ago and spent his youth here. There is a legend which still survives concerning him and his home. It is said that the saint, apostle of the Indies, was travelling to the Far East in company with the king's ambassador and they went through Pamplona. The castle, Xavier's home, was quite near and the ambassador suggested to Francis that he should make the detour and visit his aged mother who was still living. He could never expect to see her again in this life.

There are two versions of the saint's answer. In the first he is made to demur on the grounds that God's servants should be detached from all human ties, and Xavier, following the gospel precept, must now '*hate* father and mother, yes, and his own life also'. In the second account he refuses to go and say good-bye because he could not face the ordeal. He loved his mother so much that 'to go home under such circumstances would only unman me'. He will wait till he reaches heaven and then he can see her and the rest of his family and remain with them without fear of any cloud casting a shadow on their joy.

The Jesuits at Xavier Castle told me that the one thing certain about the whole story is that it is a myth, a fabrication pure and simple, invented by some pious biographers, scores of years after the death of the saint. The simple fact is that Xavier's mother was no longer alive on the occasion described.

None the less the story seems worth the telling. Both accounts of Xavier's alleged reluctance to visit his home illustrate a trait which actually did exist in his character. For Xavier had in him what Mary Purcell would describe as 'some streak as unyielding as the iron ores with which his beautiful land is seamed'. Yes, the Basques are tough. They are a hardy people, 'charged with the accumulated energies of generations whose lives are a ceaseless, stubborn conflict with the sullen breakers of the Cantabrian coasts'. When the terrific potential in Xavier was directed towards the acquiring of holiness, when he applied himself to co-operate with God's grace with all the fiery ardour and unremitting perseverance of his race, is it any wonder that he emerged a leader of men, a master-phychologist, a diplomat, a man combining the most exalted experience of the mystical life with a thorough grasp of practical problems of his day and an amazing tact and skill in handling them? St. Ignatius said that Xavier was 'the toughest clay I ever had to handle'.

Xavier Castle is set on rising ground. It stands out in splendid, defiant solitude, dominating the vast plains which stretch for miles all around its feet below. A climate such as this would be bound to produce a character used to physical endurance, obstinate in opposing difficulties, loving an argument, not easily shifted from a position once taken, courageous in facing kings or emperors to plead for and defend the cause of Christ, impatient of delay, finding it difficult to be tolerant of the apathy or pride or stupidity of those working under him, 'a saint in a hurry'.

He wrote back from India to Ignatius and told him of the urge he felt to go around all the universities and colleges of Europe and cry out, in the anguish of his heart, to so many who were sitting complacently in cushy jobs at home, when the immense harvest of souls in India was ready to fall into the hands of the harvesters, if only they were there to reap it.

Xavier's life within the castle walls would certainly have seemed austere, especially from the viewpoint of our days of central heating, electric light, carpeted floors, television and luxury armchairs. The large living room had no fire, even in the depth of winter; the walls were bare, and, by our standards, rough and unfinished; the tiled floor was cold under the feet; the chairs were hard and uncushioned and perpendicular; the fare was plain if plenteous. It is clear that Xavier would, early in life, have habituated himself to take discomfort in his stride, a most valuable asset during the years of fatigue and toil which lay ahead.

People wrote back, years later, from India: 'We have a priest out here named Francis Xavier. He is like a man beside himself with love of Christ and love of souls'. I said Mass in the castle here, just as it was said, four hundred years ago, in the same spot. If the door had opened behind me and creaked, and curly-headed, bright-eyed eight-year-old little Francis Xavier had tip-toed in, he would have felt himself completely at home.

You could almost see them there gathered round, the father Don Juan and his wife Mary; Magdalene, the future

Poor Clare nun, to whose sound advice it was due that Francis was not recalled from his studies in Paris; Miguel and his brother Juan who fought on the side of the French against Ignatius Loyola at the siege of Pamplona. At that time Francis was only eleven. Had he been a few years older he might have gone to the wars and perhaps his hand would have hurled the cannon ball by which Don Inigo was laid low!

From this castle Xavier went off to Paris to study at the university there. He was probably all agog with excitement at the prospect of seeing life, and, maybe, happy enough to shake off the exacting demands of the discipline established at home. People showed me the rock where he is said to have halted his horse, turned around to face the castle and waved to his mother who stood in the turret, watching him till he was out of sight. In some such way did Mary, too, stand one day at the door of her kitchen in Nazareth, as her Son walked down the sloping street to go out into the world to preach the Good News.

Little though Dona Maria or Francis suspected it, the parallel was very close. Xavier did not know; the lonely mother whom he was leaving behind in that vast solitude did not know; but a young man was on the threshold of a career which would tower far higher than any man can dream of. Francis Xavier was going out to set the world on fire with the love of God.

Father Saez, my English-speaking friend, left Xavier Castle on the same morning as I did. He was taking a group of boys to Madrid in the same station-wagon which had brought me to the castle some few days earlier. Leaving the castle, they hoped, with luck, to get into Madrid at about nine p.m. So many hours couped up in a wagon! Tearing along over bumpy roads! I offered at once to accompany them, and so it was arranged. Later, however, Father Saez, with many apologies, explained that there would not be room and asked if I would revert to my original plan and travel by bus.

I feel sure Xavier would have invited himself to a seat in that wagon. He would have enjoyed the bumps and would have joked about the general discomfort. He would have been the life of the party and the youngsters would have forgotten the length of the road, as at one time he sang with them and invited them all to join in the chorus. At another time he would entertain them with marvellous stories and here we may be sure he would include the stories of the saints, and his listeners would begin to wake up to the fact that the saints were mighty heroes, men and women, whom Xavier's audience might well wish themselves to be. You may be certain that they all sang from time to time in chorus, and I can see Xavier beating time with both arms raised. They prayed together too and enjoyed whatever meal they were offered. If any of them got tired, as well they might, Xavier would do everything possible to settle them comfortably and urge them to have a good sleep if they could.

If this aspect of his character is correct and from what we do actually know of it, I think it is fair to suggest that it is, then we would add that Xavier was ahead of his time. I say that because at a recent function, I saw a priest who would be about Xavier's age at the period we are picturing him, and all I can say is that his friendliness and patience and courtesy would incline me to think he was Xavier's twin, only that the saint did not have a twin and he died 400 years ago.

In 1956 I got a surprise letter from the bishop of Fargo, North Dakota, U.S.A. It was a most cordial invitation to come out and visit his diocese and work there for a while, after which, if I wished, I might move on elsewhere to find further missionary effort. He was certain many retreats and missions would come my way; these had been the main field of the apostolate in which I had been working since my ordination.

I read out the letter from the bishop for Father Byrne, my Provincial. His immediate comment was: 'Accept that invitation by all means'. I should add that I had two cousins, Presentation Sisters, in that diocese. They had been given permission to come home for my ordination. I more than suspect that it was they who nudged His Lordship and gave him this brilliant idea.

So I had a year in the States, during which I travelled much, spoke much in private conversations, in missions, and in retreats. I came home, laden with pages of notes regarding my experiences, notes which, to my shame and sorrow, I cannot find anywhere now.

I said in another place that I have always been more interested in people than in places. I propose to indulge this preference once more, in what I have to say about my trip to America.

My choice is a Carmelite nun who lives far away from all the noise and wealth and pleasures in which her country abounds, deliberately and eagerly choosing to live in silence and solitude, alone with God.

The girl was popularly known as Billy. She was the only child of very wealthy parents who idolized her and spent lavishly on her education. The world was at her feet. She was a very beautiful girl. She graduated brilliantly. She played the piano and sang charmingly. She was popular everywhere, at parties and shows, and many a young man had to swallow a lump in his throat when he looked at her, wanting nothing so much as that she should return his glances.

Her parents were Catholics, sound in their faith, but by no means enthusiastic. They had ambitious plans for this lovely girl of theirs. They would be satisfied to allow her to choose her own career and agreed to co-operate in it with her, whatever it might be. One morning at the breakfast-table Billy dropped a bombshell! She told her father and mother, straight-out, with no introduction to prepare them for what was coming, that she had made up her mind to become a Carmelite nun.

Her father stared incredulously right in front of him. Her mother relaxed into her chair and feared she was on the edge of a nervous breakdown. Had the girl taken leave of her senses? A nun, of whatsoever brand, was bad enough. But a *Carmelite*? One of those strange beings who lock themselves in behind bars, knowing nothing and caring nothing for all the really good things in life! It was unthinkable. Somehow or other Billy must be disillusioned, not to say exorcised.

Finally, after endless discussions, her father came up with a new idea. 'Billy,' he said, 'your mother and I think you should pack up and go off to Europe for a year. Enjoy yourself. Go wherever you like. Do whatever you want. Meet what people you choose. See everything. But for heaven's sake get this crazy notion out of your head before you come home.'

That was how Billy came to Dublin and met a Carmelite nun there. 'I told my story to a Carmelite priest in Clarendon Street, Mother', she said, 'and he advised me to come along and have a talk with you'. She repeated that same story that day to Mother and promised to call again on her return from the continent. Mother told her to pray much to Our Lady and to the Holy Spirit, to direct her in this very important choice. She would be praying with her and would look forward eagerly to meeting her soon again.

She came back after a few months and gave Mother a graphic and enthusiastic account of the wonderful time she had had. 'And now, Billy, what comes next?' Mother wanted to know. 'What next? Why, Mother, you should not have to ask. I'm going back home and right into the Carmelite Convent. My good father and mother sent me on this trip hoping the fine time would at least shake my vocation; more, half expecting that it would rid completely in me what father called my crazy notion. The exact opposite has happened. I enjoyed the sights and the people and the interesting things I learned. But in the midst of all the fun I used to feel a great emptiness in my heart. It is all so futile, so superficial, so fleeting, compared with the stable, peaceful, tranquillising effect one experiences when God makes His Presence felt. I would not and could not dream of anything only to consecrate myself to Him alone'.

To their sorrow and keen disappointment her parents soon saw that the plan had failed. The only effect the trip had on Billy's resolve was to make it stronger than ever. Father got one more idea and he clung to it like the last straw. 'Billy', he told her, 'since you are so determined about this, you can have our permission and approval, though very reluctantly granted. We lay down only one condition, that you enter the Carmel in Santa Clara'. That convent was six hundred miles from home, and her parents hoped against hope that Billy would soon get lonely and come back to them. This device also ended in failure. If Billy had been given her choice it would have been Santa Clara, precisely because it was at such a distance. She wanted to be 'alone with the Alone', and she felt that Christ wanted the same.

So, to Santa Clara she went. Little did I ever dream that I would come there and give a retreat to her community, meet her in person, and hear the whole story from her own lips. She told me of the terrible pain she had endured by clinging to her resolution. She loved her parents dearly and it did so hurt to cause them such anguish and disappointment. Of this she gave no indication at the time, fearing lest any suggestion of yielding might make them indulge in false hopes.

Of course they love her still and of course she loves them. But 'he who loves father or mother more than Me, is not worthy of Me'. This is one of the 'hard sayings' of the gospel. Through God's grace Billy rose up to the ideal it demanded.

One short sentence she spoke to me comes back to my mind: 'You know, father, we have *everything here*'.

What did she mean? Certainly not the pleasant way of life which she had tested and found wanting. What she meant is that she had proved for herself the truth of St. Paul's words to the Corinthians: '*In all things* . . . you are made rich in Him . . . so that *nothing is wanting* to you in any grace'. Like St. Teresa, the great mother of Carmel, this devoted daughter of hers can repeat, with deepest conviction: 'Jesus Christ is my all . . . without Him all is nothing to me'.

This is something much more than a mere assent. It is what Newman would call a 'real' assent, in contradistinction to a 'notional' assent. Billy always believed in Christ and that He is God. But immense light was given to her to probe very deeply into the actuality of this knowledge. In that light she believed but also *realized* three magnificent truths about Christ.

First, Christ is the source of her interior life, the life of grace in her soul. She understands that the more she grows in this grace the holier she will become. Hence her one desire and resolve is to maintain constant union with Christ, like the branch in the vine, and by virtue of this uninterrupted contact that *interior life* of grace will go on increasing as long as she is in this world. This, very briefly, is what is meant by saying that Jesus is the source of her interior life.

He is, secondly, the model of her *exterior life*. Her exterior life is made up of the actions she performs, the words she speaks, the tasks she engages in – everything, in fact, which occupies her in the life which people see her living. In all this she checks her conduct by what she learns about Christ's exterior life, and her one holy ambition and desire is to do and work and speak and rest and treat others and react to every circumstance, as He would do. 'Be ye imitators of me', says the apostle, 'as I am of Him'. How would Christ reply to this question, handle this situation, take this meal? He becomes her greater self, her model in all exterior things.

Finally, He is the inspiration of her *apostolic life*. This means, that, having learned by personal experience His lovableness in her relations with Him, she longs to share with the whole world the treasure she has found, the blessedness of belonging entirely to Him.

She has become 'Christified', changed, in a manner, into Christ living in her, directing her, urging her by the constant promptings of His Holy Spirit to spend herself and be spent in the most divine of all divine works – the salvation and sanctification of souls.

Christ is the source of her interior life; the model of her exterior life; the inspiration of her apostolic life. Well indeed might she tell me: 'Father, we have *everything* here'. Only one person can stand at the centre of a circle. You can place as many as you wish round about if you make the circumference wide enough. For Billy, Jesus is unique. He alone occupies the centre. All others, all occupations, plans, works, desires, are subservient to Him. 'What is not God is to me nothing'.

This wonderful intervention of grace fascinates me. I felt compelled to tell the story. Perhaps the Lord had some special purpose in moving me to do so. Who knows but that it may fall into the hands of another 'Billy'?

Says Father Monscheur, in his book *Christian Prayer*:

> More and more has the view been accepted that the mystical life of grace which reaches its apex in contemplation, rightly belongs *to every child of grace*, because it is, in reality, nothing else than the perfection of the three theological virtues, faith, hope and charity, within us, infused at Baptism, and God Himself deepens and strengthens and kindles them within us . . . Always, however, this presupposes that the soul has been faithfully submissive to the gentle, guiding direction of the Holy Spirit. It is this fidelity, we repeat, which constitutes our contribution, and God demands it.

We have heard of Lourdes and Fatima and Knock. I get the impression that the story of Our Lady of Guadalupe, Mexico, is not as well known in our part of the world as it should be. Even if I am wrong in thinking this, I do not hesitate to pick out at least the salient points, to remind ourselves once more of the immense graces Mary can communicate, using the weakest and, by human standards, the lowliest instruments.

In this case the instrument was a poor illiterate Indian named Juan Diego, who lived with his wife a hand-to-mouth existence in a remote section of the hill country known as Tepeyac. The Franciscan Fathers had penetrated this far and Juan and Maria Lucia, his wife, had accepted, with the simplicity of little children, everything they had learned from them. They went regularly to Mass, though this meant a journey of more than fifteen miles there and back, on foot and over rocky surfaces. There were no children and when his wife died Juan nearly died of grief after her. For Juan, about fifty by now, the loneliness was unendurable. He could no longer bear to go on living in the same place haunted by memories of her wherever he turned. To effect this plan to live elsewhere was the thought most often uppermost in his mind.

One Sunday morning he was making his way with difficulty across the fifteen miles which separated his home from the church. He shivered in the bitter December weather. Suddenly he stopped dead, rooted to the ground. Mary was standing a few yards in front of him. She beckoned to him to come towards her. He felt no fear, only intense delight and wonder, marvelling at her exceeding great beauty. She told him he was to carry on with his journey to Mexico city and tell the bishop that it was her wish that a temple should be built there, 'to be a witness to my love, my compassion, my succour and my possession'. Juan bowed low and answered: 'Lady, I go to do your bidding. As your humble servant I take my leave of you'. With all speed he hastened down the slope of the hill to Mexico city and the house of Fray de Zumarraga, the Franciscan who had become its bishop.

The late Francis Johnston, ardent lover of Mary, whose love for her he was skilled in breathing into everything he wrote about her, has helped to immortalize the story of poor ignorant Juan, describing for us the many trials and labours her faithful servant had to face up to, and the ultimate success, little short of miraculous, with which he accomplished his task.

On arriving at the bishop's palace the bearer of Mary's message was insulted and beaten up by the servants. He was refused an interview with the bishop and only his dogged insistence finally gained for him a grudging permission into the presence of His Excellency. His Excellency was not favourably impressed. The poor Indian meant well no doubt, but he was probably allowing his heart to run away with his head. But he was a troublesome fellow, maintaining that he had seen Mary and that Mary had unquestionably given him this commission. All right. Let Juan go back and ask her for a sign to prove the truth of the story. Little did His Excellency suspect the challenging answer Mary would give to his demand for proof.

Juan went home and found his uncle seemingly dying. He hurried back to Tepeyac, where he had seen the Lady, but he avoided the spot where he had met her, fearing she would come again and delay him. That would not do, for he had not a minute to lose if the priest was to reach his uncle in time. But she pursued him and he explained with delightful child-like simplicity that he could not delay, in view of the imminent death of his uncle. 'Please forgive me, dear Lady. I promise you faithfully to come here again tomorrow'.

Our Lady replied, in words which have resounded in many a heart ever since. 'Listen, my dear little son. Do not be troubled or weighed down with grief. Do not let any illness or vexation or anxiety or pain disturb you. Am not I here who am your Mother? Are you not in the folds of my mantle? What more can you need? And I tell you, further, to have no worry about your uncle for he is cured at this moment'. This sublime message was spoken not only to the lowly, unknown Indian four hundred years ago. The words are for each of us and they will be a source of joy and courage and gratitude, in all sorts of circumstances, if we just make them our own.

And what about the sign asked for by the bishop? Mary told him to return in the morning to the spot where he had first seen her. There he would find an abundance of beautiful flowers growing. He was to gather some of them into his apron, or tilma, let no one see them till he got into the presence of the bishop. Then let him open his apron and show him, and tell him this is the proof provided by the Mother of God.

Early next morning he was at his post. He stood there rooted to the ground in blank amazement. An exquisite profusion of flowers, blooming on the frozen ground, sending out a delicious fragrance! He filled his *tilma*, opened it to show Our Lady what it contained. She arranged the flowers with her own hands and sped him on his mission.

There was more trouble about gaining admission to the bishop, but Juan was determined. After about an hour's delay he succeeded. He repeated his story, adding, 'and here Your Excellency, is Our Lady's answer to your request for a proof.' The flowers fell in abundance on the floor, filling the air with their fragrance. But that was not all. When finally the bishop succeeded in withdrawing his gaze from those flowers he looked at Juan's tilma. So did they all and instinctively they fell on their knees. Juan turned his eyes in the direction of his apron and to his astonishment saw on it an exact replica of the Blessed Mother as she had shown herself to him on the mountain.

Little did I ever dream, when I read this story for the first time, that I would one day have the privilege of climbing up to the heights of Tepeyac, in the footsteps of Juan, and offering the holy sacrifice in front of the tilma with the image of Mary as visible upon it today just as it was four centuries ago.

I have written only the most meagre introduction to the story. Miracles multiplied. When Pope John Paul II visited Mexico in 1979 he stood in front of Juan's tilma, in a densely-packed basilica with more than a million gathered outside. He spoke out of the fullness of his great heart:

> Ever since the time that the Indian, Juan Diego conversed with the sweet Lady of Tepeyac, you, Mother of Guadalupe, have entered decisively into the Christian people of Mexico. To all, you utter those gentle and inspiring words: 'Am I not here who am your Mother?'.
>
> O Immaculate Virgin Mother of the true God and Mother of the Church, you who from this place reveal your clemency and your pity for all those who seek your protection, hear the prayer that we address to you with filial trust, and present it to your Son, Jesus Christ, our sole Redeemer. Mother of mercy, teacher of hidden and silent sacrifice, to you, who come to meet us sinners, we dedicate on this day all our being and all our love. We also dedicate to you our life, our work, our joys, our infirmities and our sorrows. Grant peace, justice and prosperity to our peoples, for we entrust to your care, Our Lady and Our Mother, all that we have and all that we are.
>
> We wish to be entirely yours and walk with you along the way of complete faithfulness to Jesus Christ in His Church . . . Hold us always with your loving hand.

We have often asked Christ to teach us to pray. Go to Guadalupe and learn. Let me recall briefly a few out of many scenes which I saw. Many young men were there at six in the morning, on their knees, dropping in on their way to work, just exactly as you might see them at home. They dumped their tools on the ground beside them, jerked the lunch they carried under their arm into a more secure position, and then, with hands joined and eyes raised, gave you your object lesson in the art of communing with God in prayer. High up above them all, to reach which you must climb about forty steps, there is set, in the midst of lights and flowers, the very *tilma* worn by the humble Juan Diego, still bearing upon it the miraculous image of Mary. Statues of Juan and Bishop Zumarraga flank the altar on both sides, statues of white marble. Juan in his peasant's dress and surrounded by Castilian roses. He seemed to reach across the centuries to the little saint of our own day who promised that, after her death, she would let fall a shower of roses.

A little girl made her First Holy Communion at the Mass following mine. She had a special prie-dieu in the sanctuary, and one for father and mother on either side. Before he gave her the Gift of God the priest came down, stood close and delivered a short sermon all for herself. She knelt there in her flowing white gown and white veil, with eyes cast down, motionless all the while, the most self-possessed child you could wish to see. She received with exquisite reverence. The priest, when I questioned him afterwards, did not know even her name! I had been deciding that she must be the daughter of a duke or a count. I was wrong. She was a princess, daughter of the King to Whom she had just given a royal reception.

I want to slip in here a thought which sometimes worries me. I feel that in preparing our children for first Holy Communion too much stress is laid on the externals – the white dress and gloves etc. – and that there may be a real danger that the child's mind is so engrossed by these that he or she may neglect to lay the emphasis where it belongs – on the wonderful love of Christ who is coming into our souls.

During his visit to Mexico the Holy Father reminded the people that half the number of Catholics in the world are in their country.

We begin this section with an invitation to the reader to sit down, in spirit, with a group of Jesuits having their evening meal. The place is still Mexico. Presently the priest next to me asks me, in Latin, if I understand what the talk is all about. I shake my head and answer 'not a word'. Then he goes on: 'The fathers are saying they think there is one Irish priest here in Mexico. If you wish we shall try to find him for you'. That was how I found myself, half an hour later, at one end of a phone, thrilled to hear Father Tom at the other end wishing me a céad mile failthe to Mexico. His grand Dublin accent, especially in this vast city where I was a complete stranger, echoed in my heart like the sound of music.

I felt even at this first contact with him that he was just as well pleased as I was and my subsequent meetings confirmed this impression. He came for me next morning and proved himself to be a veritable angel guardian to me during the rest of my visit. It is the function of an angel guardian to direct and guide us aright and Father Tom made me feel like Chesterton's man who leaped on to his horse's back and rode away at once in all directions! He left nothing undone to let me see Mexican life from every angle and to introduce me to Mexican friends of his from every walk of life.

But that was far from being all. He fascinated me and delighted me and edified me profoundly by his living faith and boundless zeal. His full name is Father Tom Fallon. At forty-seven when living in Dublin, he had heard about the need for priests in Mexico. He wrote to the Superior of the Missioners of the Holy Ghost and ultimately went to join them and was ordained. The ceremony was performed during the height of the Calles persecution, in a small room in a private house. Archbishop Diaz, a Jesuit, the first archbishop of Mexico, raised Father Tom to the priesthood – his first priest.

He brought me into a small chapel, and pointing to the tabernacle, he whispered: 'This marks the spot where the head of the holy soul rested when she was dying'. He was referring to Concita, a married lady and mother of seven children, whose beatification now seems certain. Father Phillipon, the distinguished Dominican theologian, was enthralled by the beauty and sublimity of her very many writings. He declared them to be theologically sound and he confessed himself to be utterly astonished to find such loving familiarity and such frequent communications between God and this soul. She was raised to heights of contemplative prayer comparable to those of the greatest mystics, such as St. John of the Cross or St. Teresa.

Father Tom loved to talk about her. I can still catch the tone of reverence and awe with which he pronounced her name, 'the holy soul'. To have known such a soul, to have directed her, to have shared her heavenly communications, was, for him, a very special grace. If she is canonised, and her Cause has moved far, it will be particularly gratifying to remember that she was a married woman with a large family, whose marvellous gifts of prayer never prevented her from giving the most conscientious attention to her home and family.

She left behind her a host of manuscripts. They reveal to the world the inexhaustible riches of the Cross and of the mysterious dealings between God and this His chosen servant. Her mind was marvellously illuminated to see deeply into the perfections of God, her heart went on fire with love at the vision that was shown to her, and she committed it to paper in a language which clearly echoes the promptings granted to her by the Holy Spirit of God. 'She has become, through her apostolic zeal and her heroic immolation, the spiritual mother of a multitude of souls, who, as she did, want to walk in the footsteps of Christ to be crucified with Him and to save men with Him.'

As in the case of Father William Doyle and Eamon Murphy of whom we have written elsewhere in My Last Book, a Jesuit cannot but be happy to record that what Conchita regarded as 'the central grace of her spiritual life' was granted to her while she was making the 'Spiritual Exercises' under the direction of a Jesuit.

It is difficult to refrain from giving here, the sublime correspondence between her Jesuit son Manuel and herself when he wrote to her from Spain that, after much prayer and direction, he had volunteered for a foreign mission and so she would never again see him in this life. She replied:

> Tearfully I offered up to God infinite acts of thanksgiving for having given you the strength to carry out so great a sacrifice. I went up to the tabernacle and put your letter close by it. I bore it over my heart on the next morning when receiving Communion, to renew my full acceptance.

Happy are you, my dear son, for having placed Jesus above flesh and blood, for having known how to raise yourself in an aura of faith above this earth. Oh, Manual, son of my heart, that which is the greatest thing after God, the sole divine thing a creature can do, is to love Him and glorify Him in sacrifice of himself. St. Ignatius' motto is the supreme formula of love: *To the greater glory of God.*

Before we read the weighty words which are to follow, it will be well to remind ourselves that Conchita is no alarmist or sensationalist. She is a woman whose writings have been solemnly approved by recognised authority, her communications with God in prayer have been pronounced authentic, and the process of her cause of beatification is well in hand. I say this so as to stress the fact that her words cannot be dismissed lightly. Here they are:

If souls lag along the road and their interior life is extinguished, it is the priest's fault. The gates of divine communication, opened for the mystical life, are closed. Why? Through apathy . . . through dissipation of their lives, through their lack of mortification, through their neglect of study in this domain, through absence of close and conscientious rapport with souls, through their want of the spirit of sacrifice because they do not love enough. Here are the causes: Lack of prayer, of the interior life, of purity of soul, of intimate relations with Me, absence of love, and devotion to the Holy Spirit, of union with God.

The transformation of the priest into Me which takes place in the Mass, he must continue in his ordinary life, in order that his life be interior, spiritual and divine . . . The world opens at this moment a large breach in the hearts of priests and you know the number of vices which accompany this redoubtable enemy; an excessive contact with creatures chills their fervour, the neglect of external and interior recollection brings tepidity. Hence, when the world enters, the Holy Spirit departs. When the Holy Spirit leaves the heart of a priest he is ruined, for if anyone has, not only the need but the most imperious obligation to live and breathe in the Holy Spirit, it is the priest. To the measure by which He departs, materialism penetrates. Woe to the priest who founders himself in matter! He can consider himself lost. This is so easy in a dissipated soul, in a heart which does not pray and is not mortified.

Father Miguel Pro S.J. was only three years ordained, when, after a long series of hair-breath escapes, he was finally seized by the Calles Government in Mexico, put standing against a wall and shot dead. He was a Jesuit, and the Jesuit charged to promote the cause of his beatification has high hopes that soon he may be honoured on our altars and possibly even be declared a martyr.

We visited his grave, of course, Father Tom and I. He is buried at the 'Dolores' cemetery, but one must not allow the name 'Dolores' to deceive. The grave of Father Pro shouts out joyousness and victory. 'Let us say the *Te Deum* here', suggested Father Tom. And, indeed, what else could we do, unless, perhaps sing it?

Plaques and medallions and inscriptions are all over the place, expressive of the gratitude of hundreds of people who attribute miracles to the prayers of this great priest. The flow of visitors is continuous. I remember seeing a tall, handsome young soldier, who stood at attention for some minutes in dignified silence. Then he knelt and prayed, touching the 'martyr's' grave with his rosary.

Spies and secret police dogged Father Pro's footsteps everywhere. As a student in Europe and while living in his own country as a young Jesuit, he had proved himself unsurpassed as a finished actor. 'I have a habit of ragging', he once wrote. His companions remember him as a born wit. He would act in plays and concerts in his community and bring the house down.

Little can he have imagined in those carefree days that his gift would be used magnificently to save him from many an arrest and to extricate himself from many a tight corner.

He borrowed all sorts of clothes to disguise himself. He passed for a young man about town, in grey flannels and open-necked shirt, with a broad-rimmed bowler hat, cocked on his head at an angle of forty-five. Sometimes he would allow his moustache to grow and sometimes shave it off. He was possessed of consumate skill and courage to carry off a situation perfectly. He thought swiftly, acted, and always managed to do the right thing.

He had three big operations as a student which caused him agonies of torture. On the eve of the third one he wrote:

> 'Take all from me Lord, only give me souls. In wealth and fortune and honour, let me have no part. Only give wings to the devouring flame that zeal and love of Thee have lighted in my heart.'

Right in the heart of the persecutions, this prodigious

priest conducted enclosed retreats for taxi-drivers, for ladies, for school and college boys, even for Government officials, and often within a stone's throw of Government buildings. The Reverend Father Director would arrive in a smart suit, with cigarette, and flower in buttonhole all complete. 'Would that I could multiply myself a hundred times over', he would say.

He was everywhere, bringing Holy Communion, preaching, absolving, comforting the sick and the dying, saying Mass, inspiring courage in face of fierce odds. From the small hours in the morning till any time at night this went on. Food? Sleep? He didn't seem to have a thought bothering him about such trivialities. Was his inexhaustible energy supported by some miraculous strengthening from God? Read the life of this amazing man and you will not be surprised at the suggestion.

Once a group of Catholics had gathered secretly in a private house for Mass. The spies got wind of it and when Father Pro arrived he found two policemen standing guard in front of the door. He stuck out his chest, assumed an attitude of vast importance, produced from his breast-pocket a notebook and pen, examined the number of the street and checked it with what was supposed to be in his book, then glanced at the house. 'Something fishy going on here, eh?' Then, half raising the lapel of his coat to indicate he was wearing underneath an officer's badge (which wasn't there), he walked right in. The two constables sprang to attention, clicked heels and saluted as he passed. And, in the most casual manner in the world, Father Pro acknowledged the salute, walked in, and let his congregation out by the back door!

Another day he realised he was being shadowed by two of Calles' worthies. On turning into a street he recognised a Catholic girl, he winked at her, grinned and took her by the arm. All the discomfited police could figure out was a pair of lovers, strolling together arm-in-arm in lovers' lane!

There was dire poverty everywhere and he put his pride in his pocket and begged. 'You cannot imagine the shame there is in begging, always begging', he wrote. 'Happily the One for Whom one does it is not parsimonious'. Once he got into a bus carrying six live chickens; another time he walked through the streets encircling a live chicken in his arms, and a live turkey to boot! The people laughed and so did Father

Pro. No one suspected the inner struggle he had with his natural pride.

'So far', he writes, 'I have eighteen families provisioned for two months. I do not know how, or when, or from whom, but one day I get fifty kilos of sugar, another time boxes of biscuits, chocolate, rice, and even wine. And the Providence of God is so fatherly that when I am just scratching my head and asking myself to whom shall I go and beg from, I find that the room is well filled up. May Jesus be praised! I have not time to breathe, I am in work up to the neck, giving food to the hungry, and they are many. My purse is as flat as the spiritual part of Calles, but that is not worth a thought, because the Overseer in heaven is so magnificent'.

His last retreat was given to a group of working men, among them three shoemakers who assured him that what he said fitted their feet to perfection. All declared that the retreat was 'a great profit to the constituent mentality of the nation'. 'I didn't quite grasp their meaning', said the priest, 'but their hands I grasped with such fervour that mine smelt of cobbler's wax for three hours'.

He was bound to be caught unless Satan had gone completely out of business. On November 15th, 1927, two bombs were thrown at the car of General Obregon, a minister of Calles. In the questionings which followed the name of Father Pro's hiding-place was accidentally divulged. The priest was sleeping there, and also his brother Humberto, when the police arrived. Since the attempt on Obregon he had moved about with even greater freedom and daring, convinced that the pursuers, preoccupied with the search for the assassins, did not have time or leisure to bother too much about himself. It never remotely occurred to him that the assassination could possibly be attributed to him.

Yet that was the charge. The police ordered him and Humberto to rise at once and come along. Before they left, Humberto asked his brother to give him absolution, and he did, despite the prohibitions and protests of the head of the police. They were charged with the attempt on the life of the General, and, further, it was they who were responsible for the throwing of the two bombs. This was news and they did not hesitate to say so. They were flung into prison. On the morning of 23rd November, just a week after the arrest, they were taken out into the garden, placed by the wall facing the firing squad and shot in cold blood, without trial.

Had he any last request, the priest was asked. Yes, that he might be permitted to commend his soul to God in prayer. For two minutes he knelt, profoundly recollected, and then, perfect master of himself, he rose to his knees with the dignity and bearing of a saint, his eyes alight with the eager expectation of very soon fixing them on the King and Queen he had loved and served so loyally.

Unhurried, the priest asked to be shown where to stand, then took up his position and drew from his pocket his rosary beads and his crucifix. It was his Jesuit crucifix, such as every Jesuit receives on the day of his vows. He extended both arms full so that his body formed the figure of a cross. In his right hand he clasped the crucifix and with his left he held his beads. He stood there before them unflinchingly. He was not blind-folded and his gaze was fixed calmly on the five rifles levelled at him. In tones vibrating with the intensity of his love he exclaimed: 'Live, Jesus Christ the King!'

A minute later and Father Miguel Pro had once more effected an escape, only to be captured again immediately by the divine Hound of Heaven. Escape is now no longer a possibility. Father Pro is a prisoner for life, a prisoner of love. The winds which blow from his grave bear with them the germs of a life that is indestructible, germs which, finding a fertile resting-place in Mexican soil, will yield fruit a hundredfold.

About four hundred lepers were there, on the settlement some forty miles outside Mexico city. Father Tom brought me to visit them at my own request. We presented a card to poor Avelino, which he took into his badly-twisted fingers. It was from one of the Jesuits, asking Avelino to show us around. About half the people on the settlement are Catholics.

Avelino's case was far from being the saddest. He could at least hobble about and he was able to occupy himself usefully with work on the large adjoining farm. But what about the poor man of seventy, confined to bed for the past ten years, his eyes blinded by the disease and his left leg rotting away progressively each day? His room was a dingy hole, with bed linen ragged and dirty. All day and all night there he lies, perfectly conscious, his mind quite clear, and himself completely dependent on his fellow-lepers to feed him and wash him. I can still see the two of us standing there looking helplessly at him. Father Tom said a few kind words in Spanish. We gave him our blessings and promised to pray for him. And he promised to pray for us.

You could not but recall the gospel story. The sight of this poor man helps us to understand the urgency with which lepers implored Jesus to cure them, once they had heard of His power. 'Lord, if Thou wilt, Thou canst make me clean. Jesus, Son of David, have mercy on us'. In those days lepers were compelled by law to cry out: 'Unclean, Unclean', if a stranger appeared, and no one ever touched a leper. I touched some of them as we moved from one to another, in the effort to try to express my sympathy. I could see that my doing so astonished them. Father Tom whispered, 'Don't father. They don't expect it, and you never know what might happen!' The implication smote my heart with terror. I remembered St. Francis fleeing in horror at the sight of a leper, and then, filled with shame and remorse, returning and kneeling before him and kissing his sores.

Even more vividly does my visit to this place recall the heroic story of Father Damien of Molokai. In his early years he studied for a commercial profession, but as a result of a mission given by the Redemptorists he entered the Congregation of the Sacred Hearts of Jesus and Mary. In due time he was ordained a priest. At a conference presided over by his Provincial he heard the ghastly story of the lepers on the island of Molokai. Moved by the Holy Spirit he volunteered to go out and live in the midst of them. His offer was accepted and, on 10th May, 1873, a historic date in his life, he disembarked at the island, stepped ashore, and served the poor people soul and body for twelve years without a break, till his death.

There were about six hundred lepers on the settlement at Molokai. By Government orders they were segregated from all contact with anyone outside. Father Damien, burning with zeal and compassion, became not only their priest but their servant. He dressed their sores, helped them to build their cottages and went so far as to dig their graves and make their coffins. He returned to his little house one night, after a strenuous day. He heated some water to bathe his feet. When he put them into the basin he felt no reaction. What that meant he knew only too well. Next morning he addressed his people, using the phrase: 'We lepers . . .' Soon he became helpless and went to His God to receive the reward of his heroic sacrifice, which he made, not merely without complaint but with the Christlike love in his heart which, like all love that is genuine, expressed itself in deeds.

Leprosy, like every other ill that flesh is heir to, is traceable to sin, which might be called leprosy of the soul, because it destroys sanctifying grace, which is the soul's sharing in the very life of God. This is, beyond all comparison, the major calamity.

If there had been no sin, this colony would never have existed, and these poor people would not be afflicted in this terrible manner. If leprosy such as we saw it, be the fruit which stems from this root, what must the root itself be? Leprosy corrupts the corruptable body which must of itself disintegrate anyhow, but sin stifles and kills and degrades the life of the soul. 'Man, when he was in honour, did not understand. He compared himself to the brute beasts and became as one of them'.

St. Catherine of Siena used to know when a person in her vicinity had mortal sin on his soul. Either he or she had to leave, because she found the stench to be unendurable. When the prophet casts about for a metaphor by which to describe the sufferings of Christ, what he writes is that: 'He became, as it were, a leper'.

A priest dropped in to see me. We were both in Jerusalem, members of a pilgrimage organised by Mr. Michael Walshe, who honoured me with an invitation to come along as spiritual director. 'I'm going to admit', said the priest who visited me, 'that this is an overpowering experience. Don't you feel awe-inspired when you stand before the altar for Mass, and say to yourself: "This is the very spot. This is where He was actually crucified for my sins. Mary stood beside the cross, right where I am standing at this moment".'

It is the same wherever you go. The whole atmosphere is charged with the clinging memory of what He did and why He did it and how; of the words which fell from His lips and the tone in which they were spoken. He looked down along those streets and walked barefoot over those stones. He climbed this mountain and knelt here to pray.

A few days earlier I had driven in from the airport and got my first glimpse of this city seated upon the hill. The sight is not prepossessing. The hill is barren and stony, with scarcely a blade of grass to be seen, and you tell yourself that its forbidding aspect accords well with the crime forever linked inseparably with its name.

But in fairness to Jerusalem it must be stated that, if our first reactions were unfavourable, they were soon to be changed profoundly. The voice of our driver broke in on my reflections. 'If you look over there, about half a mile to your left, you will see the garden of Gethsemani and the Church of the Agony. Right behind the church, on both sides, stretches out the valley of Cedron, topped by the Mount of Olives, from which Christ ascended into Heaven. The mosque of Omar stands close by. The church? That is the church of the Holy Sepulchre and it covers the spot where Jesus was crucified and buried, and rose from the dead.'

Impossible to convey in cold print the effect of words like these, even when spoken so mechanically and suggesting no appreciation whatever of the depths of meaning they contain. Is it all a dream? Are these the very streets which echoed to the sound of His voice, as one time He pleaded with men to seek their peace and happiness in Him alone, or spoke words of stern and uncompromising condemnation of their sins, or of warning to repent while yet there was time? In meditating prayerfully on these questions and answers lies the all-absorbing interest of the true pilgrim to the Holy Land.

I felt simply compelled to give some account of this experience in my last book. I took copious notes, and fortunately, unlike others I made elsewhere, they did not get lost in transit. Indeed, they are so numerous that my difficulty will be what I shall be forced to leave out.

It will be most profitable for my readers, I think, to give

one or two incidents in some detail, rather than gloss over a large number and leave nothing behind but a confused impression.

So, let me please begin with an account of an experience I had at the time and which grips me and has the same effect on me every day or night when it comes to my mind. That evening our group gathered together into the church of the Eight Beatitudes, on the north-western side, close to which there was a hostel where we were to spend the night. It was here that Our Lord, early in His Public Life, gathered a crowd around Him, and 'opening His mouth', He preached what has since come to be known as the Sermon on the Mount. The walls of the church are octagonal in shape, with one of each of the eight beatitudes engraved on them. It was my privilege to deliver 'a sermon on the mount' in the exact spot where the Master had taught the crowds.

Afterwards I walked down to the shore. I discovered an old unused shack, where I sat, protected from the wind, looking at what was right in front of me. I felt that the urge to pray was irresistible. I watched the full moon creeping slowly up behind the hills and moving out into a cloudless blue sky. It was reflected perfectly on the surface of the lake at my feet, which lay there, motionless, without a ripple, like a huge mirror. Thank God the hand of man cannot change those hills or those waters. I drank in the beauty till it filled my whole soul. This was the stillness, the peace and tranquility one longed for.

I looked over to my left. There was the hill where He had gone up to pray. I could almost see Him dismissing the crowds, starting the climb, His shoulders slightly bent forward, gathering the folds of His white cloak with His right hand, and, on reaching the summit, pausing for a moment, joining His hands, falling on His knees to speak with reverence in the sight of His Father, enveloped in the rays of the moon shining down upon Him. The whole world and its trivialities seem so senseless up here. Here one touches realities as one contemplates Christ in prayer, His whole being plunged into that sacred act, His heart on fire with love of His Father, and of us, and of me; His anxiety for man's true interests lending zest to the prayers He pours out, for me and for all men.

I have tried to reproduce the scene I saw so vividly on that wonderful night, and for a special reason. Most of the readers of my last book, I imagine, will be men and women who take their religion seriously. I feel great confidence that if they would sometimes slip away into a quiet corner in church or home, and kneel in spirit with Christ as He prays this night, they would taste and see how sweet the Lord is. 'Sometimes the best kind of prayer is just to kneel down and let Him look into my heart.'

When next I turn my eyes in the direction of Christ over there in prayer, I notice a slight movement in the hitherto motionless figure. He rises from His knees, walks down swiftly along the slope, and without in the least slackening His pace, he walks across the waters. He had ordered His apostles to get into the boat and row across to the other side. A fierce storm had swept down suddenly upon them. They were terrified, as well they might be, and it did nothing to lessen their fear to see this object in white walking towards them. A ghost, surely. No. Not at all. 'Only Jesus', telling them that there was nothing to fear and bringing all safe back to the shore.

The story of that night and the feeling of that atmosphere I love to reflect upon. I only wish I had the gift to communicate to my readers the sense of reality it brings. It needs to be re-lived in a prayerful spirit, and, indeed, the main purpose of this chapter is to try to communicate in other incidents too how this can be done.

Let me see how I can assist at the Last Supper in this prayerful spirit. The room where it was held was upstairs, reached by an outside staircase. I see Christ and His twelve apostles climbing those steps and moving into the room. They sit at the table, Jesus in the middle. I follow in after them and I walk boldly right up the full length of the room till I come to the table, directly in front of Christ. I kneel down on the side opposite to Him, rest my hands or arms on the edge of the table, look at Him there in front of me, look at them all, and, in this perfect setting, with all my powers focussed on what is going to happen I begin to pray.

There are three mighty truths here. The first of these is: *such a gift*. I believe, I am certain, that what seems to me to be there lying on the table is the living Body and Blood of Jesus Christ. I believe, not because I understand, but only because He says it. God is as really and truly here, on that supper table, as He is in heaven. There is one difference only. In heaven the souls believe because they see Him as He is, face to face, and the vision transports them with love and joy which will never end. But the *reality* is as truly on this supper table as it is in heaven. God can do all things, but here, so to speak, He is taxing the powers of His omnipotence, and stunning me with amazement.

What am I to pray for in this first part of my meditation? Surely for a more living faith which will send light into my dull mind and awaken me to reality. Christ said: 'How long a time have I been with you and you have not known Me?': The day I even begin to know Him in this sacrament must revolutionise my whole life. I can never be the same again. Let me stop reading now and ponder prayerfully over the gift I see on that table. Let me say, again and again: Lord, increase my faith.

My next thought is about the precise circumstance of *time* at which he gives such a gift. Kneeling here at the table I look around at His friends. There is Judas with his horrible secret. This very night he has laid all plans to betray Christ. And Christ, knowing this, retaliates by giving Judas such a gift at *such a time*. There is Peter who is going to deny Him three times this very night. And this very night He gives Peter such a gift. And, as far as the rest of them are concerned, this very night they will all scamper away in terror at the first sign of danger. Would I present a television set to a false friend of mine on the very evening I had learned that he had blackened my character?

Such a gift, at such a time, and now, *given in such a manner*. Jesus surrounds the giving of His gift with every circumstance calculated to impress on the group at the table, that He is giving it for one only reason, because He loves, and love wants to express its love by giving. In what manner does He give? He begins by kneeling in front of each man and washing his feet. That was why Peter remonstrated so strongly. Jesus then sits down again and opens His heart to pour out an inexpressibly beautiful address. He is saying to them: You do not know how much I love you. You do not know how ardently I long for you to love me. Finally, you do not know how much I want you to love one another.

It is all true. It is all real. I simply must stay here, and come back again and again to this table. A Protestant said to a Catholic friend of mine: 'If I believed what you Catholics believe about the Eucharist, I think I would never be off my knees'.

St. John tells much of this extraordinarily beautiful story in chapter 14 and 15 of his gospel.

Another unforgettable experience was our public holy hour in the garden of Gethsemani. All of us, I suppose, had often made a holy hour before. But this one was absolutely unique. Other holy hours we had made during a retreat, or in the privacy of our own little room with the door closed in on Him and ourselves, or perhaps at some public shrine, Lourdes, Knock, Fatima.

But the holy hour that night in Gethsemani had this incomparable feature – that we were making it in the exact same spot where it had first been made by Christ. In front of the altar there is a large piece of rock against which tradition says Jesus had knelt for support during His agony. The surface is smooth and shining as a result of the millions of pilgrims who have come there to touch it and kiss it ever since the first holy hour when Jesus had leaned against it as He prayed.

On leaving the supper room we walked with Him to this garden, following literally in His footsteps. On the way He had repeated for us the three great truths about love, so as to sow them deeply in our hearts. *You do not know how much I love you. You do not know how much I want you to love Me. You do not know how much I want you to love each other*. He had just had time to finish what He wanted to say as we walked into the garden. 'I will not leave you orphans,' He had assured us. 'As My Father has loved Me so do I love you. Abide in My love'. We caught our breath, so as not to miss a single word of this astonishing assurance. If only we realised its depths and its meaning as the saints did!

A change comes over Him as we enter the garden together. He begins to tremble. His eyes are stark with terror. He rests His right hand on my shoulder needing my support. He begins to speak and His words are muttered slowly and with obvious effort. 'Stay with Me', He implores. 'Watch with Me. My soul is sorrowful even unto death'. He drops on His knees under the olive trees. I can see Him only confusedly in the light of the moon shining between the branches. He falls flat on His face. Not knowing what to do I drop on my knees beside Him. I lay my hands on His shoulder, at least to try to keep Him from trembling. My hands! They are wet! I stand up, come out into the full light. I turn up the palms of my hands. They are red, red with the blood of Christ forced out of the pores by some agency of which I am ignorant.

As I stand there staring at those hands of mine, I catch once more His words, scarcely audible. 'Father, if it be possible, let this chalice pass from Me. But Thy Will not Mine be done'.

With utmost reverence let me kneel and take into both my hands this chalice of which He is speaking figuratively. The gospel tells me it contains three bitter ingredients. I look into the cup and the first ingredient is *fear*. 'He began,' we read, 'to be afraid'. No wonder, for the terrifying vision breaks in upon Him of the unspeakable sufferings of mind and body now about to fall upon Him. There is the mockery, the jeering, the night alone in a dark dungeon, the mock trials, the obviously false accusations, the hatred of the mob, the corruption of His judges, the scourging and crowning of thorns, the road to Calvary and the meeting with His mother, the unspeakable agony for three hours on the cross. And, running right through all this, the hatred, the jeering, and the seeming uselessness of it all when at last His head falls forward in death.

When next I look into the bowl of that chalice I find that the second ingredient is disgust or utter loathing, (*taedere*). What causes this? The vision of sin, of all the sins of all time which He has come to expiate. Who can understand sin? Only God Himself, because only God understands His own unutterable holiness, against which sin is degrading, nauseating, the son or daughter of God lowering self to the level of the beast and becoming like them. The world takes sin in its stride because sin is pleasure. But pleasure and happiness are not the same. Jesus shrank back in disgust. He had to atone for all the sins of all time. What the vision caused Him shows us, as nothing else can, the true nature of sin.

Lastly, 'He began to be sorrowful and to be sad,' because, despite all He was about to do for sinners, some would be lost in hell. How many? He was asked that question but He refused to answer. All He would say, and it supplies material for many an hour of prayer and meditation, is the following solemn warning: 'Strive to enter in by the narrow gate . . . few there are who find it'.

No more zealous and dedicated apostle of the Holy Hour could be found greater than the late Archbishop Fulton Sheen. He tells the story in a chapter of his autobiography which he calls: *The Hour Which Makes My Day*. I wish I could incorporate every word of it into my last book. I can only tell you that every day of fifty-six years this great priest never once missed that continuous holy hour of prayer before the Blessed Sacrament such as we made it on that memorable night in Gethsemani. 'I am convinced', he writes, 'that our people are searching for the old devotions which many of the parishes have done away with, and this is very often because the priests cannot be bothered putting themselves out'.

His chapter on the Holy Hour is enthralling. Here is one quote:

> The purpose of the Holy Hour is to encourage deep personal encounter with Christ. The holy and glorious God is constantly inviting us to come to Him, to hold converse with Him, to ask for such things as we need and to experience what a blessing there is in fellowship with Him . . .

Archbishop Sheen was a brilliant scholar. Remembering this, the childlike simplicity revealed in the following passage is all the more moving.

> As a teacher in the Catholic University in Washington, I arranged to put a chapel immediately inside the entrance of the front door of my home. This was in order that I might never come in or go out without seeing the sanctuary lamp as a summons to adore the Heart of Christ at least for a few seconds. I tried to be faithful to this practice all during my life, and even now, in the apartment where I live, the chapel is between my study and my bedroom. Even at night, when I am awakened and arise, I always make it a point to drop into the chapel for a few seconds, recalling the Passion, Death, and Resurrection of our Lord, offering a prayer for the priests and religious of the world, and for all who are in spiritual need. Even this autobiography is written in His Presence that He might inspire others when I am gone to make the Hour that makes life.

I must leave it to my readers to imagine what the experience must be for a priest to stand on the Hill of Calvary and offer the sacrifice of the Mass there. Says the author of the *Imitation of Christ*: 'A priest wearing sacred vestments takes the place of Christ, humbly and earnestly to beseech God for himself and for all His people. Before him and behind him he wears the cross on the chasuable that he may gaze earnestly on the steps of Christ and ardently desire to follow them. He wears the cross of Christ behind him that he may bear, without retaliation and for God's sake, whatever injuries are done to him by others. He wears the cross in front of him that he may grieve for his own sins, and behind him that he may mourn in sympathy over the misdeeds of others, remembering that he has been set as a mediator between God and the sinner'.

Before telling my readers how it came about that I went to Rome to meet the Holy Father, I must preface what I have to say by a page or two regarding a group called *Action from Ireland*. We told you already that it is a small organisation committed to social action in Ireland and in the Third World. It believes that the Arms Race, costing over *£800,000 every minute*, is not only highly dangerous, but morally unjustifiable in the face of World Poverty. Here follows a brief statement of the facts. We, here in the Northern Hemisphere have one-third of the world's population. The Third World, with a population of more than double ours, has to try to exist on *one-eighth* of what we use for ourselves. May I ask our readers please to go back on this paragraph again in order the better to understand the galling injustice involved?

Don Mullan, the first national director of *Action from Ireland* came to see me here in Gardiner Street, where I live, about two years ago. He wanted to pour out for me, with intense conviction ringing in every word, the story of what may be called the major attack of Satan on the world and civilisation. In the interval I have come to respect his judgement, his grasp of the relevant facts, and the sound projects he plans to launch and has successfully launched, in the effort to cope with the present situation. At the stage I have now reached I think I might say I am convinced that he has been given a special vocation from God analogous in many ways to my own vocation to the Society of Jesus. He is loyally supported by a group of men and women who are deserving of the same eulogy. Readers looking for more information will be given it gladly if they contact Action from Ireland, Third World Centre, 86 Summerhill, Dublin 1. Phone: (01) 724632.

Serious-minded men, thoroughly-well informed, warn us that it may be the end of the world. Our Holy Father told the United Nations' Assembly:

> The life of humanity today is seriously endangered by *the threat of destruction* taking the risk that sometime, somewhere, someone can set in motion the terrible mechanism of general destruction. We must ask ourselves whether there will continue to accumulate, over the heads of this new generation of children, the threat of common extermination, for which the means are in the hands of the modern state.

Cardinal Manning of Los Angeles writes:

> There are in existence at this moment, in the hands of the superpowers, weapons of war that include fifty thousand nuclear bombs, two hundred of which, were they detonated, would destroy all the largest cities in the world in one hour. Our culture is a dance of death. We are fast approaching the pig-level of the Prodigal Son in the mercy parable. But the end may not be yet. From the cinders of our burnt-out world God can still raise up children to Abraham. Then, from its ashes will rise a new heaven and a new earth.

The people living in the Third World are God's children, our brothers and sisters, to be loved and helped and prayed for, for this reason more than all others. It is so dreadfully possible to look at a shocking scene on our television screen and be moved for the time being, and resolve vaguely to do something about it, and forget all about it when the next item comes on. The seed remained lying on the surface of the soil, waiting to be blown away by the next gust of wind. We need to live with our eyes open. What is wanting is, even more than financial aid, a change of heart. This means that we realise we are faced with a situation, the challenge of which is not only a matter of choice but a grave obligation.

Jesus tells us about a wealthy man named Dives. He kept a good table. He dressed elegantly and expensively. He probably regarded himself as a very respectable citizen. We are not told that he was immoral or cruel or unjust. But from Christ's own lips we learn that that rich man died 'and was buried in hell'.

Why? Well, at the gate leading up the avenue to his grand house, there sat an unfortunate beggarman, shivering in his rags, starving for a morsel of food, with no companions but the mongrels who nosed round about him, licking his sores. Likely enough Dives used to drive past him in his car. He would cast a contemptuous glance in the direction of the poor man and mutter to himself that the fellow was an eye-sore. Dives would have to arrange to have him pushed into some institution for receiving paupers and loafers.

It was true that the tables up in the house of Dives were groaning under a load of food. It was true that the 'left-overs' after the rich man's dinner would have tasted like a feast. It was true that Dives had a wardrobe stuffed with expensive clothes, more than sufficient to last him for three times the number of years he was likely to live. But it just did not occur to him to hand over some of the cast-offs to cover the frozen body of his suffering brother and restore some warmth into his shivering limbs. That sort of thing was not done. He only let the poor man die; that was all. But for just that much alone 'the rich man died and was buried in hell'.

I confess I never read that story in St. Matthew's sixteenth chapter without a feeling of anxiety, and sometimes of deep pity, for those who have too much of this world's goods.

In the fiftieth year of my priesthood I visited Rome.

The highlight of the trip was my meeting with the Holy Father. I had the privilege of con-celebrating Mass with him in his private oratory one morning, and of having an audience with him afterwards. I had jotted down a few things I wanted to remember to say to him, and he listened as if he and I were the only two people in Rome. He commented and asked questions and sent blessings. He presented me with several rosary beads blessed by himself. He embraced me and wished me' 'Happy Jubilee, Father'.

About an hour before this happened we were shown into

his private chapel where we found him on his knees before the Blessed Sacrament, wrapt in prayer, in preparation for Mass. It was good to know that the Holy Father gives a full hour to prayer before his Mass and some twenty minutes afterwards. I felt comforted to recall that I had always strongly recommended this to priests when giving them retreats. I confess that I found it difficult to take my eyes off him as I looked over to him to observe him praying. The vision comes back to me again at this moment – Pope John Paul II, kneeling motionless, wrapt in God.

The Mass itself he celebrated with the profound reverence which flowed out from the depths of his spirit of living faith. It was a sermon in itself. A clergyman prominent in the Anglican Church – I cannot remember the name – once attended a Mass in a French Church. When he came out he said to his companion: 'I find it impossible at the moment to decide whether Catholics are right or wrong in what they believe the Mass to be, but I will say this – that priest we have just seen at the altar, he, at least, believes what he is doing'. Nobody could watch Pope John Paul II celebrating the holy sacrifice and not say the same.

It was great to meet him personally afterwards, but I wrote when I came home: 'What I really wanted was to have him all to myself, in a small room, with the door locked from the inside, the key in my pocket, and the receiver off the hook of the telephone!'

On reflecting on that encounter with the Holy Father since my return to Dublin, my imagination began to work on a scene which, though quite fantastic, might help my readers. Imagine yourself receiving a letter in the morning from Msgr. Magee, the Pope's Secretary, telling you the astonishing news that Pope John Paul II is coming on a second visit to Ireland. Incredible! But you have read nothing yet. Read on. Msgr. Magee goes on to say that the Holy Father will be remaining in Ireland for three days and that it would be a great pleasure for him if he could lodge in your home while he is here.

You will have different reactions – amazement, joy, gratitude, a feeling of unworthiness. Next you begin to plan preparations. The best room, of course, but it must be painted and papered and new curtains put up in the windows. And when he finally does arrive you can scarcely contain yourselves when you see the Vicar of Christ, in his spotless white cassock, stepping out of his car and advancing towards you, smiling and with arms extended in blessing.

It is only a supposition. But the fact it is meant to illustrate surpasses it infinitely. This fact, if realised, would bring a joy into our lives, habitual, so intense, as to seem almost impossible to bear. What is this fact? It can be stated in a single sentence: If, at this moment, I can lay my hand on my heart and say that I am in the state of grace, I can most confidently add this statement: 'The Three Divine Persons of the Blessed Trinity are living in my soul, Jesus in the Eucharist making me His tabernacle.'

Let me analyse that statement. My intimate, familiar guest this time, is not Pope John Paul II, not an angel, not even Our Lady herself. God it is Who is living in a most real way in my soul. 'If any man love Me, My Father will love him, and *We* will come to him and make our abode with him'. We have the divine assurance that 'the kingdom of God is within you'.

The Pope would be remaining only three days. How long will God stay? Why, as far as He is concerned, what He eagerly hopes for is that He will never go at all. To convince us of this, He uses, time and time again, the word 'abide'. To abide means to take up permanent residence.

Because He is always at home, I can speak to Him in all sorts of places and at all sorts of times. It is not necessary even to make an appointment. 'As the branch cannot bear fruit of itself unless it *abides* in the vine, so neither can you, unless you *abide* in Me'. When this abiding presence begins to be appreciated in my life I shall be like someone moving out of the shadows into the full daylight of an early summer morning. We might, perhaps, borrow Newman's phrase to describe it as 'the mystery of divine condescension'. With much sorrow we have to admit that many of us remain all our lives ignorant of this sublime truth, treating the divine guest so casually, ignorant and forgetful of the imminence of His presence within us. Who would treat the Pope like this?

During his years as cardinal in Poland the Holy Father had a very faithful and loyal house-keeper who served him for eighteen years. Asked what impressions he had made on her, she stressed, as the dominant one, his habitual, astonishing calmness of manner. Never in all that time did he show, even once, any sign of impatience or hurriedness. It was, indeed, often enough that he got good reason for annoyance, as when a car due to arrive to take him to an important meeting would turn up at his house half an hour late. When finally it did arrive he would walk down and sit in, unhurried, asking no explanation of the delay, giving the impression that he must, somehow, not have even noticed the delay.

This same self-possession was very much in evidence during his visits to Ireland and Britain. He moved, with perfect ease of bearing, from one situation to the next, gentle, imperturbable at all times. There was one occasion especially when this was more than usually evident. It occurred, if I remember rightly, at Glasgow, when the cheering young people could not be quieted for at least ten minutes or a quarter of an hour. The cheering would break out afresh each time the Pope showed he was on the point of beginning his address. He did not even raise his hand or try to talk them down.

How is it done? My own guess is that this man lives lovingly and habitually aware of the Presence of the Blessed Trinity all around him and in the innermost places in his own soul. 'If any man loves Me, My Father will love him, and we will come to him and take up *Our abode with him.*' 'In Him we live and move and have our being.' Pope John Paul II is a contemplative in action, vividly conscious of that divine indwelling, never wholly distracted from it, even when overwhelmed with work. He is a recognised exponent of the teaching of St. John of the Cross, the saint who teaches insistently that prayer and work must not exclude each other. Rather, they must intermingle, each complementing the other, each compatible with the other.

We found that we had to prolong our stay in Rome by two days. We were delighted. At about the same time we discovered, almost by accident, that there was a convent of Mother Teresa's nuns about twenty minutes' walk away. We could have easily missed it. Thank God we didn't. Their work for the poor is beyond all praise. We saw it in the homes they have for homeless men, in hospitals and homes where babies and small children are lovingly cared for, in refuges for unmarried mothers – no one is neglected. It is not only the care lavished on all who are poor or in need by those devoted Sisters, but the obvious joy and love with which every task is performed.

What is the explanation? I once asked Mother Teresa. 'Father, we tell every girl who considers coming to us that she will often have tasks to do which are repugnant to human nature. Let her but penetrate through the disguise and remember that she is touching the Body of Christ and her difficulty will vanish.'

Mother Teresa started her great work by picking up a little abandoned child in the streets of Calcutta. That was over thirty years ago. Her apostolate since then has embraced thousands of neglected souls all over the world. Girls are coming to offer themselves, literally by the hundred. At the moment there are over two thousand professed nuns, over 400 novices, and about 250 postulants. And this is a time when so many religious communities, both men and women, are complaining mournfully that no subjects are forthcoming.

How account for this? Father Daniel Lord gives us the answer in one of his books. He describes the methods by which visiting priests told the boys about the Order to which they belonged. That priest invariably drew a blank who painted a rosy picture in which life, on the whole, was soft and comfortable. There was no challenge. But the response was excellent when boys were told that the life was demanding, calling for courage and steadfast endurance, which was gladly borne for the sake of God.

I cannot but feel that herein lies the solution to the problem of decrease in vocations, if only we priests and religious have the generosity to accept it in our way of life. Any form of religious vocation, in the measure in which it strives to reduce the gospel teaching to literal acceptance, will find the answer to the riddle of life. Those of us religious who assiduously cultivate the cult of softness and complain that novices are few, might listen to Father Lord and take a leaf or two from the book containing the principles of spiritual training on which Mother Teresa brings up her daughters and sons. Then, perhaps, the novices might begin to knock at our doors again.

It is worth trying.

8 Uncanonised Saints

No priest of experience can doubt that in the course of his ministry he has come across men and women who would seem to have reached a degree of saintly holiness. He has witnessed the long years of painful sickness, borne, not only without a complaint, but with a patience not short of heroic. Often as he sits in his confessional he feels that he should rise and go down on his knees, in view of the sanctity which seems to radiate from some of his penitents. The reverent familiarity of the tone of voice in which they describe the loving relationships experienced between God and themselves in prayer; the real agony they feel when they reflect on the insults flung into the face of the God Whom they love. The millions dragging out an inhuman existence in the Third World, the degradation of those who are slaves to drink or drugs or sex – all this weighs heavily on the hearts of God's close friends in a manner reminiscent of Gethsemani.

Such people are crushed with sorrow as often as they reflect on these things. Why? Because their love of Christ is so living and so intense, and their sense of the heinousness of sin so acute, that life becomes for them a close participation in the Passion of Christ. Like St. Paul they confess: 'With Christ I am nailed to the cross'. This, in turn, may well mean that they have attained to a height of holiness which might well prove to be grounds for canonisation.

I have been looking forward very much to talking about an Irish Jesuit priest of our own time who would fit into this category. For him the love of Christ was almost an obsession. He felt an ache in his heart to gather the whole world together and explain to all men what they were missing and what he had found. There were times when he nearly sank down into despair as he learned more and more of the appalling prevalence of sin.

Father George Byrne, our novice master, came into our

conference room one morning to give us a spiritual lecture. He brought with him a bulky volume which had just come on the market. The author's two first sentences were:

> This book is not a mere biography. It is a deliberate attempt to give an exposition of Catholic spirituality, particularly from the Jesuit standpoint, by weaving a commentary round a life which is at once ordinary yet heroic, full of pathos as well as humour, which begins with faithful adherence to the commonplace and ends in tragic romance.

We saw very soon that the book fired Father Byrne with enthusiasm. Here was a priest who spoke to him in his own language, who was the living embodiment of the Jesuit ideal as he understood it, and had striven for half a century to live it. That such a priest had been given by Christ to the Irish Jesuits in particular, and to all Jesuits in general, left Father Byrne grappling with words forceful enough to tell us of the joy he felt and very much wanted to share with us.

He read for us a few extracts such as this:

> Jesus is the most loving of lovable friends. There never was a friend like Him before; there never can be one to equal Him. Every fibre of His divine nature is thrilling with love for me, every beat of His gentle heart is a throb of intense affection for me. . . . He knows I am all His and He is all mine. O Jesus, Jesus, Jesus, who would not love You, if only they once realised the depth and breadth and the realness of Your burning love? Why then not make every human heart a burning furnace of love for You? I cannot deny that I love Jesus passionately, love Him with every fibre of my heart. . . . He knows that my longing, at least, even if the strength and courage are wanting, is to do and suffer much more for Him, and that were He tomorrow to ask for the sacrifice of every human friend, I would not refuse Him.

This remarkable priest was Father William Doyle and his biographer was the late Msgr. Alfred O'Rahilly.

This great priest's love of Christ was by no means mere lip-service. His biographer describes many sacred relationships between Christ and His priest upon which it seems almost a desecration to raise the veil enclosing them. He writes:

> In spite of all my unfaithfulness, Jesus has given me a deep, personal love for Himself which has broken down every barrier of fear, and, perhaps what others call reverence. The happy moments I have spent up close to the tabernacle, with my head resting against it, or my heart pressed to His! I love often to clasp

> my arms round His statue and lean my head on His shoulder as St. John must have done, and give Him those marks of affection He seems so eager to receive. Oh if only we could sink into that ocean of love stored up for us in His adorable heart, eternity would not be too long to thank Him for the joy that life of love would bring us.

Msgr. O'Rahilly gives a most satisfying and balanced appraisal of what we might be tempted to regard as mere emotionalism. He writes:

> Doubtless there are stolid souls who will not appreciate these emotional outpourings, who regard such fervent language as mere sentimentalism. It is true, of course, that such utterances were never meant to be dragged from their sacred privacy into the cold light of print. But that is just the beauty of them. They well up spontaneously in the heart of a strong man, they express the pent-up enthusiasm of this brave soldier of Christ, seeking an unconventional outlet. Father Doyle was no sickly sentimentalist or hysterical weakling. He lived what he felt, and he meant what he said. Why should we fancy that strength must be short of tenderness? Why should we think that only earthly love is privileged to have its delights? Paul, the man of action, was accused by some Corinthian converts of being 'beside himself'. 'If we have been beside ourselves,' he answers, 'it was for God; if we are now in our right senses it is for you. For the love of Christ overmasters us – reflecting that as one died for all, then all were dead, and that He died for all so that the living may no longer live for themselves but to Him that died for them and rose again'.

We have had a glimpse of the depths of love on the side of Christ for his priest and the response on the side of the priest. It is only a glimpse. There are many pages in the *Life* devoted to accounts of this very marvellous, mutual affection which took place in these visitations. Here is Father Doyle's account of one of them:

> Last night I rose at twelve, tied my arms in the form of a cross, and remained in the chapel till 3 a.m. I was fiercely tempted not to do so, the devil suggesting that, as I had a cold, it was madness and would unfit me for the coming mission. Though I shivered with cold, I am none the worse this morning; in fact the cough is better, proving that Jesus is pleased with these 'holy follies'. At the end of an hour I was cold and weary. I felt I could not possibly continue, but I prayed and got wonderful strength to persevere till the end of the three hours. This has shown me what I might do, and how, with a little determined effort, I could overcome the greatest repugnances and seeming impossibilities.

Such stories have always made sensible people like ourselves raise our eyebrows. This is especially true today when we talk about doing our own thing and when the cult of softness and being yourself are the slogans which have largely taken over. There are dangers in self-imposed penances. The underlying motive may be a secret pride, like the pharisee in Our Lord's parable who boasted that he fasted twice in the week and gave tithes of all he possessed. Such deeds, praise-worthy and meritorious as they could be, lost all their merit in God's sight because the motive underlying them was pride.

Blessed Henry Suso, the Dominican, had a large collection of instruments of penance in his room. It was described as an arsenal. He was merciless in using these instruments to inflict pain on his body. One day he seemed to realise that this was full of danger; that perhaps it was only pride which was urging him to do it. Whereupon he collected all his whips and chains and hair-shirts and dumped them into the Rhine, telling the Lord he would leave it to Himself what to impose or not to impose. Very soon he was publicly accused of a serious moral fault. He was entirely innocent but the charge proved to be a much more demanding penance than all the contents of the arsenal.

There is another consideration. Christ Our Lord redeemed us by voluntary suffering. He need not have done so. Because He was God, His every act was infinite in value. Had He so chosen, He might have come into this world as a full-grown man and offered for our redemption a single prayer, one drop of His precious blood, one sigh from His heart. That much would have been superabundantly sufficient to redeem us an infinite number of times. Why, then, did He do it in the hard way? Simply because love is like that. He might have satisfied the demands of justice by taking the easy way, but love would be proved supremely by the hard way of the Cross and Passion.

For a man like Father Doyle, consumed by the love of Christ and the desire to imitate Him, nothing will satisfy his craving to express his love except, as far as possible, to live with Christ on the Cross. St. Paul stands by, ready to approve and encourage. 'With Christ I am nailed to the cross, through which the world is crucified to me and I to the world.'

This is what Christ did. This is what Christ invites us to do.

We can be adept at inventing specious arguments to justify ourselves for toning down this hard saying. Let us admit this much at least. Msgr. O'Rahilly writes: 'There is no detour around the hill of Calvary'.

Before finishing my scrappy account of this great priest I turned to the concluding pages of his biography. I found it nearly impossible to lay aside, and now that I have at last succeeded in doing so, I have a still more difficult problem to solve. What to select and what to include from those glittering pages to give my readers even a few flashes of light which shone out over his last years, a fitting climax to the inspiring story which I have tried to sketch. It is understatement to say that there is not a dull page in this book. It is brimful of interest, the details of an inspiring life, a challenge to our spiritual apathy and sloth. It pulverises all our specious arguments about moderation and commonsense; it must reveal to us, if we are honest, our cowardice; it charges us with frittering away so much of God's precious time; it condemns us for the readiness with which we stifle the voice of conscience urging us, even at the eleventh hour, to begin to take seriously the work of becoming saints; it takes all the starch out of our pride and leaves us limp and humbled and fearful as we look back over the myriad of neglected opportunities.

But it will do more. It will burn into our minds and hearts that golden sentence from Blessed Claude de la Colombière: 'It is well worthwhile striving to become a saint, even if you were assured you had only a quarter of an hour to live.' God is not limited by laws of space and time. Many repentant sinners have found a niche for themselves in the ranks of the uncanonised saints.

Father Doyle became an army chaplain during the 1914-18 war. He was killed by a shell on the 16th of November, in 1917. Here are some of the things people had to say about his work among his men, and about the love, greater than which no man hath, that he lay down his life for his friends.

> Father Doyle was one of the best priests I ever met and one of the bravest men who have worked or fought out here. I recall the early Mass when our battalion was in reserve. Often have I knelt at the impromptu altar serving Mass for the padre in the upper barn, hail, rain and snow blowing in gusts through the shell-torn

> roof. He knew no fear. Many a dying soldier on the bloody field has flashed a last look of loving recognition as our brave padre rushed to his aid, braving the fearful barrage and whistling machine-gun bullets, to give his boys a last few words of hope. Utterly fearless, always with a cheery word on his lips, and ever ready to go out and attend the wounded and dying under the heaviest fire.
>
> If I had gone through one-thousandth part of what Father Doyle did, or if I had taken a hundredth part of the risks he ran, I would have been dead long ago. Wherever there was danger, there was Father Doyle, and wherever Father Doyle was, there was danger. Whenever I saw him coming I told him to go away as I knew the enemy would shell the place at once! When shells were raining on us, he used to wander about, from dug-out to dug-out, as if he were taking a walk for the good of his health. Everyone in the battalion, Catholic and Protestant, idolised him. He loved his men and spent every hour of his time looking after them, and when we were having a fairly hot time he would bring along boxes of cigarettes to cheer us up.

The priest himself writes:

> Ah, Father Doyle, Father Doyle, whispered a dying man, and he motioned me to bend down lower. He put his two arms around my neck and kissed me. It was all the poor fellow could do to show his gratitude that he had not been left to die alone and that he would have the consolation of receiving the Last Sacraments before he went to God.

We round off this section with Father Doyle's last message to his father:

> I have told you all my escapes, dearest father, because I think that what I have written will give you the same confidence which I feel, that my old armchair up in heaven is not ready yet, and I do not want you to be uneasy about me. Leave will be possible very shortly, I think, so I shall say only *au revoir* in view of an early meeting. Heaps of love to every dear one. As ever, dearest father, Your loving son, Willie.

'Before this letter reached home,' says Msgr. O'Rahilly, 'the great Leave Day had come for Willie Doyle. He was called Home. "Blessed are the dead who die in the Lord that they may rest from their labours, for their works follow them." '

Sarah Benson had a tiny shop, almost directly opposite the parish church in Borrisoleigh, Co. Tipperary. I got into the habit of dropping in for a word, when passing her little home, on my way to and from the church during the mission. I think she owned the house and it was as well, for what she had to sell could hardly pay a small rent and at the same time provide enough food to keep her alive. She exhibited for sale a few loaves, lemonade, candles and sweets!

So in one sense she was poor indeed. But, according as I got to know her, I discovered a wealth so vast that the riches of an Onassis or all the kingdoms of King Solomon would seem to be little more than a handful of sand by comparison. For Sarah, I am convinced, was an 'uncanonised saint'. I was persuaded of this from the occasional glimpse I got into her interior life and the outward expression which showed itself in her daily way of living.

Naturally speaking, her simple, uneventful existence should have been dull and boring. Yesterday was the same as today, and tomorrow would be a repetition of today. It never occurred to Sarah that there should be anything different. She was loved by everyone. She welcomed all visitors with a bright smile and a cheery word. She was one of the most even-tempered people I ever met. Whenever she spoke about herself – it was not often – it was only to praise and thank the good God for forgiving all her sins.

Her best friend was living only a few hundred yards away, Christ in the Blessed Sacrament. There was daily Mass and often during the day she would drop in to tell Him how much she loved Him. On these occasions she would always wear her shawl on her head and shoulders as a mark of reverence. She had no complaints. She saw no faults in anyone except in herself. She had no thought for the morrow. Her needs were not many and *He* would be always there to supply them. And, moreover, Mary His Mother was Sarah's Mother too.

What was the secret of this unalterable evenness of disposition? It rested on the solid foundation of the three theological virtues – faith, hope and charity. She accepted the truths of the faith with the unquestioning readiness of a little child. She had never opened a book of theology, but she had an enlightened faith which many a scholar might envy her. She did not merely believe, as she might have believed in the existence of New York or the Treaty of Limerick. She *knew*. With Job she could say: 'I *know* that my Redeemer lives, and that in the last day I shall rise up out of the earth, and I shall *see* my God in the land of the living'.

Sarah had the gift of an indomitable hope in God. She fed her mind on the thoughts of the promises He had made. She was aware that human friends sometimes make promises which they conveniently forget when the time comes to fulfil them. But Sarah knew Christ her friend too well from experience ever to doubt for a moment that He might fail to do and give what He had promised. If ever she felt a sense of depression or loneliness her heart was once comforted and thrilled when she reflected on His words about the never-ending joys of heaven, and now, in her mid-fifties, she realised that she would be meeting Him soon and entering into the immeasurable blessings He had prepared for her. There may be some discomforts during the journey but what matter when she had her eye all the time on the journey's end?

Often, when she sat or knelt with Him over there in the chapel, with her eyes fixed on the tabernacle, she would tell Him how much she loved Him, and the ecstacy was so strong when she realised the stunning fact that He loved poor Sarah, that she was all but over-powered. 'I have loved you with an ever-lasting love', He assured her. 'Abide in My love.'

And what would be the last chapter of the story of this delightful intimacy between Christ and Sarah? Why, that death would be the end of the journey. At present she was like a person travelling by train, every delay along the line marking another station nearer to her destination. One day, it must be soon, the train would halt with a jerk and Sarah would stand up and look out of the window to see where they were. And the name of this station, written there in large letters for everyone to see would be: *Eternity*. All change here.

Sarah's angel-guardian, whose unseen presence never left her little shop in Borrisoleigh, will show himself to her now and accompany her straight to heaven, her home forever. Before they enter the golden gate he pauses to explain to her that she can leave the virtue of faith outside. There is no faith in heaven. It gives way to Vision, the face-to-face vision of the Most Holy Trinity, no longer hidden as in that little church she loved at Borrisoleigh. The vision of this inexhaustible beauty will become almost like an obsession, but an obsession causing a never-ending ecstacy.

Her angel reminds her too, that she can no longer exercise the virtue of hope, because she now possesses every blessing she could possibly wish for, and with that, an absolute guarantee from God Himself that there is not, and never can be, any sort of series of circumstances to endanger her possession. 'I have found Him Whom my soul loveth. I have held Him fast and will never let Him go.' What a compensation for the poverty borne so cheerfully in Borrisoleigh!

And what about charity, the love of God and the love of all for love of Him? 'Charity', says St Paul, 'never falls away'. It is the only one of the three virtues which we take with us to heaven. The love for each other which the blessed have in heaven is the overflowing of the love of God from out of their hearts and sharing itself with every other soul.

Why do we suggest that the name of Sarah Benson should be included in our list of uncanonised saints? Look back again at the small house in Borrisoleigh and reflect on the life she lived there. We find there is an astonishing similarity between Borrisoleigh and Nazareth, and between Mary's way of living and Sarah's. They were both poor. They were both sinless – Mary always, and Sarah, I feel sure, from the day of her baptism. They both governed their daily lives by the light and the love of a living faith, a strong hope and a burning love. And for Sarah, as well as for her great Mother, there is now neither faith nor hope, but only charity which never falls away.

In this sophisticated, questioning, cynical age, it is indeed refreshing to breathe the atmosphere of a childlike acceptance of what God teaches us through His Church. By a happy coincidence, this chapter is being written on the first day of October, the feast of St. Thérèse, raised up, as the Holy Father tells us, to teach us the depths of her doctrine on the spirit of little children in our relations with God. 'Unless you become as little children . . .' There is a simplicity which is filled with true wisdom.

Nazareth and Borrisoleigh had this marvel also in common, that Jesus was as close to Sarah in the church across the road, as He was close to Mary in the kitchen at Nazareth.

Frank Daly in his teens was a rabid communist. He was, he

considered, one of a worldwide group of dedicated men and women, profoundly affected by the sight of the squalor and misery everywhere and determined to wrest from the hands of the greedy wealthy their vast possessions and distribute them among the poor and the homeless, enough and plenty for all. He had been brought up a Catholic, but as soon as he began to think for himself he became aware that it, too, looked without pity on the desperate condition of those who were dragging out, day after day and year after year, an existence approaching nearer to the life of an animal than of a human person.

But delivery was at hand. Frank knew it and thrilled to the challenge it offered him. He talked about communism wherever he went. After a while he tried his hand at writing articles and he was bloated with pride when these were accepted by editors with strong approval and a request for more. Frank was on the crest of the wave. He would have thanked God for it, but in the light given him in the communistic creed there was no God. There was contempt for those too blind to see that God is dead.

On one memorable day Frank wrote about communism in an article which he considered to top all others which had gone before it. He was jubilant. He would mail it forthwith. But he would entrust it to no hand other than his own. So he started out for the post-office with the previous document safely lodged in his breast pocket. Halfway there, he began to feel a sense of dizziness. He paused, tried to steady himself, failed, collapsed, and began to haemmorhage violently. He awoke an hour later to find himself in bed, in hospital.

He chafed at this unwarranted interference with his plans and cursed it. For a while his communistic companions came along to visit him, but, as the weeks dragged on, they grew tired and one by one dropped off. Frank lay there seething with anger and hating them for letting him down. But in his solitariness Christ came back to him. He began to recognise the selfishness and callousness of his so-called friends. This led him to recall what he had experienced of the love of Christ and His Mother in other days. Back in the religious atmosphere of his home he mellowed under the influence of God's grace. The nightmare passed and he woke up and found himself back again in the full light of a perfect day.

He was an invalid for the rest of his life. It was God's way of leading him to a marvellous growth in holiness. For the most part he was alone and in silence, and in prayer he found a new way of life. It was all-absorbing. He felt the nearness of God to him; more, the actual Presence in his own soul. Every other interest fell out of his life. This new way of life he might have summed up in the words of the canticle: 'I have found Him Whom my soul loves; I have held Him fast and I will never let Him go'.

It was about this time that I came to know him. I used to visit him in his mother's house. He had a room upstairs, devoid of all comfort, with just a few sticks of furniture and his books. It looked cheerless and it felt cold, but you forgot that as soon as you began a conversation with its single occupant.

You were scarcely sitting down, with Frank beside you, when he plunged into the one subject which alone interested him. He was not curious about news; he had long ago dismissed and forgotten the fables of communism; he was in close and constant touch with God and the supernatural and that left him with no time for anything else.

I can see him, even at this distance, welcoming me with a reverence which would have embarrassed me if I did not realise that it was being shown to the priesthood of Christ in me. He had no chair, only a bench and here we would sit and I would listen to him describing his experiences in prayer, the love it engendered, the longing it created in him to make a return of love, however hopeless the attempt might be. Moses went up the mountain and walked into a cloud where he engaged in familiar conversation with God for forty days and forty nights. 'Alone with the Alone.' They spoke to each other, we read, with the intimacy of two close friends. The description might be applied to what took place between Frank Daly and his God in the poor room where he discovered true riches. But he was on only the outer fringe of the conversation. 'We see now through a glass darkly, but then face-to-face.'

There came a day when I called. I wanted to get the courage and inspiration he always gave me by his word and example. But I did not meet him that day. He was gone from that place forever. To contact him I would have to kneel and pray with the confidence that he is now to be numbered among the uncanonised saints.

I don't know even the name of the next person who would seem to have a right to a place among the uncanonised saints. A brother-priest told me about him and there is no doubt in my mind that he was one of 'God's Own'.

This priest was walking alone, along a country road. He came upon a man seated on a heap of stones. He was smashing the stones with a large hammer which he held in his right hand. The priest stood to talk to him. In the course of the conversation he threw out the question: 'Tom, you're sitting there every day for several hours, breaking these stones. I'd be interested to know what you think of during that time when you are all alone and with no one to talk to.'

Tom pushed back his cap, dropped his hammer, and pushed his blue goggles from his nose up to his forehead, and gave the priest an answer which delighted him. 'What do I think of all day? *Father, I'm always thinking of God.* When I was a young man a missioner explained to us that, to be in the state of grace does indeed mean that there is no mortal sin on our souls. But it also means a whole lot more. He told us that it means that the Holy Trinity, Father, Son and Holy Spirit are living all the time within us. He urged us to make the offering every morning without fail, and, from time to time during the day, to train ourselves to repeat it in a brief form such as: 'All for Thee, O Lord. O my Jesus all for Thee'.

He suggested further that it might help to offer each day for a special intention, such as for persons in grave sin, for the dying, the souls in purgatory, priests and religious, our Holy Father the Pope, The Church, Peace throughout the world. I do that, father, first thing every morning adding my special intention for that day. And you see this hammer? I've made a pact with God always living in my soul, that every time I lift it up He is to accept it as a repetition of my Morning Offering.

'No, I'm never a bit lonely or depressed. I never feel short of company. How could I be short of company when all I have to do is turn my eyes in on my own soul and find God there?'

Would readers agree that the writer of the following letter might also be counted among the uncanonised saints? She very graciously allows me to reproduce it, on condition that I give no inkling as to her identity. Here it is:

> I trust you won't mind my writing to you, father, as I am sure you are very busy. I want you to know how much I enjoy your writings in the Sunday Press and in The Evening Press. My son gave me your book *Bringing Christ Back* as a gift. It surely does make one realise what Our Lord suffered for us in the passion. It makes me beg Him to forgive me for my share in causing these sufferings to Him. I am a widow. My dear husband died after five months' illness. Although I loved him dearly I am so grateful to the good God for granting him a holy and happy death, and for giving me the courage to accept it. Just before he died we had been praying around his bed, the family of ten and some friends and neighbours.
>
> I said: 'Pat, I want to thank you for the twenty-eight years of such a happy life we had together. I ask Matt Talbot and Padre Pio to take you by the hand and present you to Our Blessed Lady that she, in her turn, may present you to her divine Son, until we will all be re-united in a happy eternity. Then my brother-in-law said to me: 'He is going'. I said goodbye to him. 'Holy Mother most sweet lead him safe to the feet of Jesus.' We recited the rosary. We said the 'Te Deum' in thanksgiving for the grace he had received of a holy and a happy death.
>
> I still miss him, of course, but I am also most grateful to the good God. I trust God will accept our loneliness in union with His own loneliness in the Blessed Sacrament. In some strange way his death seems to have brought me closer to God, although I know I should love Him much more than I do, and with greater reverence in the Real Presence and in the Holy Mass.

The writer of this letter has herself been in failing health for a long number of years yet her only request was that I say a prayer for her youngest son who hoped to be a priest some day.

The next on the list of 'uncanonised saints' I propose to talk about is Eamon Murphy. He was a student for the priesthood when we first met, a member of the Society for African Missions. I plan to make this short section of the book a letter to himself, recalling to his mind the whole story of the contacts which developed between us. I am fairly confident of having the right address, but, for greater safety, I am marking the envelope *To Await Arrival.* If he is not in heaven by now I cannot doubt that he will be along soon. His angel guardian will keep this document safe for him meanwhile and hand it to him as soon as the opportunity offers. Eamon will be so overpowered by the warmth and the wealth of the welcome he will receive, so enchanted by the vision of all he sees, his heart so overflowing in an ecstacy of joy and love on meeting Jesus face-to-face, on gazing on the infinite mystery of the Trinity, so thrilled by the reception given to him by Mary his mother, so delighted to find himself greeted by the hosts of angels and of his brothers and sisters the saints, that he will not have a chance even to glance at my poor script for a long time.

Nonetheless, I feel confident that some day, when he is beginning to settle down a little in his new home, he will manage to slip away into some quiet corner, take a seat, draw the letter from his pocket, spread it out on his knees, and, with the expectant smile on his face which I know so well, he will begin to explore the contents. Here is what meets his eyes:

My dear Eamon,

You probably know that I am writing my last book. I did not undertake it in a hurry. It concerns the events of my life here in this world to date – or at least for the most part. I hesitated about doing it, not quite satisfied that my motives were all right. A sentence from the pen of St. Francis de Sales did nothing to reassure me. He warns us, in no measured terms, to be very chary of talking about ourselves. Perhaps he has been telling you. Does he think badly of me, I wonder, for deciding to go ahead with this book all the same? I hope he understands and I feel very confident that you, who knew me so intimately while we were living here on earth together, will put in a good word for me, explain to him why I have done it, and tell him with heavy emphasis that I will never do it again. This volume is entitled: *My Last Book*.

I have said this because I want you to know you are to have a place in the pages. Having written thus far I paused for reflection as to how to proceed. A very pleasing picture moved before the eyes of my imagination. I saw again the day of our first meeting when you were a clerical student soon to be raised to the priesthood as a member of the Society for African Missions. You believed your vocation would be to go out to that difficult mission-field and spend your whole life there working for the salvation of souls. A noble ideal but we both know at this stage that things did not turn out just like that.

You came to the college of your Society in the west of Ireland to make 'The Long Retreat' with a group of companions. It would last for thirty days, during which you would learn much, in theory and practice, about a small book written by St. Ignatius, founder of the Jesuits. I arrived at the same time, my Superiors having appointed me to conduct the retreat. What I experienced there remains for me one of the happiest memories in my long life. This is largely due to the fact that, during those sacred days, lived alone with Christ in prayer, a deep friendship developed between you and me. It has continued to ripen ever since, and please God, it will reach full maturity when we meet again in heaven.

Before I finish this letter to you I hope to add on a summary of the content of that slender volume which the saint called 'The Spiritual Exercises'. For the moment, all we need say is that we followed it closely. I do not hesitate to give as my conviction that the Holy Spirit poured out on us an abundance of light and love and zeal. This was especially true in your case. You were in your early twenties and your companions were all some years younger. This gave you more maturity, a power to grasp reality, which was less, though by no means absent, in the others. This balance and power to lay hold on what was said seemed to me a sound reason for giving you some special treatment. I did so, and the sequel will show that this was the correct procedure.

You left nothing undone to co-operate with God's grace. St. Ignatius leaves nothing to chance. Even tiny details are included in the instructions he gives. I can only say, Eamon dear, that you observed these with a cheerfulness and a thoroughness which could not be surpassed. The result was inevitable. God never allows Himself to be outdone in generosity. He attracted you almost irresistably. He drew you as the magnet draws the steel, but with one exception. The steel, when drawn, still remains only steel. The soul, drawn by Christ, and abandoning itself into His hands completely, shares in the wonderful experience of St. Paul, when he told the Ephesians: 'I live, now not I. It is Christ Who is living in me'. And again: 'My little children, for whom I am in labour again, till Christ be fashioned in you'. I know, dear Eamon, how much you relished words like these, words that were alive, quivering with life, as we prayed over them together while we were here on earth. I tremble to think of the joy they must bring you now, when you see them verified, not in thought only, but in actual fact. If you could speak to us from heaven I think your words might be: 'The eye hath not seen, nor ear heard, neither has it entered into the heart of man to conceive, what things God has prepared for those who love Him'. It was a delight to talk to you about all that was happening in our own souls and the souls of the others making that retreat. 'In Him we live, and move, and have our being.'

I would like to refer to something I remember saying to you, as the end of the retreat began to move into the picture. I told you that I never had a retreatant who could rival your spirit of dedication. I felt all through that you were not merely hearing but listening, and not only listening but assimilating the message and applying it to every aspect of your own life. For your own part you told me you felt an assurance that you could never be the same man again. The light you had seen was too strong, too illuminating, showing up this fleeting world against the background of eternity, and the sanity of sanctity in contrast to the folly and madness of sin.

I warned that you might find it very difficult to keep your priorities right when you found yourself plunged into all the distractions of a busy active life. This was not to say that you should lock yourself up in a contemplative monastery and give yourself to constant prayer. That praiseworthy vocation was for others but not for you. The precious graces received in the retreat, so far from weakening your apostolic activity, would, on the contrary, purify it from motives of hidden selfishness and in that way make it all the more productive of graces for souls. Many of the greatest saints were 'contemplatives in action', and that, it seemed to me, was what the Lord had prepared you for in giving you the opportunity to make the long retreat.

It sounded most plausible but in point of fact it was all wrong. You had seemed to have almost touched the supernatural. You had entrusted your future apostolate to the hands of Mary. You had made to her the consecration recommended by St. Crigion de Montfort.

'I have still one thing more to tell you' you said to me, smiling. 'I was as near as I could be to losing all the grace of this retreat. You see, I came here full of anger. I had no choice but to come. My Superiors ordered me. I should have made this retreat three years ago with my own group but I was ill and had to drop out. So I was told to come along here this time for it. It meant that I was going to miss a whole month of my precious summer vacation at my own home. Yes. I was furious. I would be compelled to sit out the lectures, but I would do my own sweet will in-between. I brought with me several packets of cigarettes – which was forbidden – but what did I care? I would smoke like a chimney-stack whenever I felt inclined to. I also brought a whole lot of novels and light literature as another means by which to wile the weary hours away'.

'But, Eamon, surely you never did such a thing?' I had asked you. 'No, father, you know I didn't, thanks be to God. In your very first lecture you got my middle stump. You upset my plans completely. I threw the books into my trunk and I have not seen them since. I flung all the cigarettes into the lake – this after your opening lecture. Then I gave myself heart and soul to the retreat and you know the rest.'

'But what did I say in the opening lecture which hit you so

hard?' 'You laid great stress, father, on one point – the enormous *responsibility* we were about to incur. God had called us. He had special graces waiting for us. But He would not force them on us. He left us free, but who would dare cast aside such a responsibility? Now, father, at last you have the entire story from a to z. I am horrified to think of what I might have done but intensely grateful to you, father, to Jesus and to Mary, I'll never forget that I nearly lost one of the greatest sources of grace in my whole life.'

I have kept the anti-climax of your story till the last paragraph, Eamon. You were ordained at the Christmas following the retreat, in Newry Cathedral. Soon after you left Ireland, forever. After six weeks in your mission in Nigeria you caught blackwater fever and died! God's ways are not our ways. It is some consolation to me, and not a small one, to realise that God brought us together and made me the instrument to prepare you for your final home-coming, little enough though either of us expected it at the time.

Before I put this letter into the envelope and address it, let me ask you earnestly to pray for me. I am still in the best of health, thank God, and still able to work quite a bit. But, at eighty-one plus I have no illusions. I look death steadily in the face, knowing that I can expect to be summoned to stand before my God at any moment. Hoping we shall soon meet again in heaven, to carry on those wonderful conversations about our heavenly Father, the Son and the Holy Spirit. They will be more marvellous than ever. The gift of faith which we possessed here on earth will pass into the vision. The gift of hope will be no more, for we now possess every conceivable blessing in possessing God, and this possession, different from earthly possession, can never, by any sort of combination of circumstances, be wrested from our hands, or our hold upon it be in any way endangered. This faith and hope cease at the gate of heaven, but 'charity never falls away'. It is the only one which you brought with you into heaven.

Charity is our passport into heaven. Pray, dear Eamon, that I may have it safe and in perfect order when the Lord summons me to follow where you have led.

9 The Spiritual Exercises

No one will deny our modern widespread darkness and the apparently insoluble enigmas which agitate the minds of all thinking men. St. Ignatius wrote a little book which he called *The Spiritual Exercises* and it may be confidently asserted that in his pages he has given us the answer. After his conversion he retired to a cave at Manresa, in his native Spain. He remained there for nearly a year in solitude, plunged in prayer. His heart burned within him with a vehement fire of divine love. It could not be contained. He had found the answer to the riddle of life. He had lived all these months in a state of close intimacy with God. He could no more doubt this than deny the fact of his own existence. His name 'Ignatius' is suggestive of fire and when he came out of Manresa he felt irresistibly goaded to set the whole world on fire with the love of God.

He wrote down his experiences. Readers studying them for the first time may find them dull and prosaic. The treasure does not lie on the surface. One must dig deep to find it, but when it is discovered and seen in the full light of day it is admittedly worth the effort many times over. Ignatius was no stylist. What he gives us is an unvarnished chronicle of sacred messages from heaven, and how could any language be other than halting and unequal in the face of such a task?

Later in life when he was asked why he had made some decision, he would answer: 'I learned that at Manresa'. He stated that if every record of the Catholic faith was lost beyond recovery, his believe would remain anchored to truth because of what had been revealed to him at Manresa.

St. Charles Borromeo used to say that he received his first impulse and his first real desire to become a saint and explicit instructions how to set about acquiring genuine holiness, from the *Spiritual Exercises*. From the same source St. Philip learned to esteem contemplative prayer and a life of constant union with God. St. Francis de Sales was convinced that this book saved as many souls as it contains words. Similar high eulogies might be multiplied indefinitely, very many of them from different Popes. Here is a typical example:

> The method introduced by St. Ignatius, whom We are pleased to call the chief and peculiar master of spiritual exercises . . . is an unexhausted fountain of most excellent and solid piety, a well-instructed guide showing the way to secure amendment of morals and attain the summit of the spiritual life.

It was the power of the *Spiritual Exercises* which fashioned to sanctity the two 'uncanonised saints', Father Doyle and Eamon Murphy, of whom I have written. And, of course, the supreme proof of that power is Ignatius himself, transforming the erstwhile rough soldier, no better or worse than most of his fellows, into a man consumed by the love of Christ.

What can this panacea be, for which such seemingly extravagant claims are made? Is this philosopher's stone, this goldmine, a reality indeed or a foolish dream? In this chapter of *My Last Book* I can only pick and choose among the treasures in the storehouse, hold up one at a time for us to look at, then lay it back in its place and select another and and yet another, hoping that this much will whet our appetite for more, possibly, even lead us to make the Exercises in full ourselves.

We may hope that the ideal will become real in the measure in which we make the *Exercises*, as far as possible, in the same manner as Ignatius made them in Manresa. The fundamental condition is complete withdrawal from all other occupations in order to focus our minds and hearts exclusively on the tremendous truth that this retreat is a private audience, not with Pope John Paul II, but face to face with Jesus Christ. 'I will speak to my God, whereas I am but dust and ashes.' But, what is infinitely more important, I can confidently expect that Jesus too, will speak to me, transforming my whole life under the action of His grace.

Fidelity to silence will call for a spirit of deep faith. But, persevered in, it will develop a peace, a tranquility of mind and heart, an atmosphere of stillness in which I hear God speaking to me and am given the inexpressible privilege of speaking to Him in turn. St. Ignatius calls this 'a holy familiarity with God'. To ignore this spirit of silence, to treat it as of little importance, as is done too often, means a deplorable loss of grace. 'My son, I would often speak My word to thee, if thou would'st diligently observe My coming.' Magdalene poured out a precious perfume and the odour filled the whole house. When the atmosphere is permeated by the perfume of silence there is no estimating the heights to which a loving God will raise a fervent soul.

One might compare the retreat to the private audience between Jesus and Nicodemus at night. They were alone, in familiar conversation. Apart from that there was absolute silence. Christ's words sank into the soul of His visitor. They revolutionised his whole life. He was never the same again. This has happened in an infinite number of cases, where the soul gives the voice of God a chance to be heard. 'Speak, Lord. Thy servant is listening.'

The Spiritual Exercises are for generous persons eager to follow Christ closely and to learn what are the roads leading to Him most directly. But they have the power also, to lift a poor sinner out of the mire of sin and set his feet, too, on the way to high sanctity.

Alexis Carel writes: 'The veil between the visible and the invisible world is worn thin by prayer'. Of course it is not an empty, barren silence that St. Ignatius looks for in our retreat. The *Exercises* are a school of prayer. Prayer is a conversation between Christ and the soul. We talk to Him and He talks to us. There are generous people and they, in their anxiety, try to monopolise the conversation. There can be long periods of silence during which our prayer can be very real and very intense and a bearer of much grace to our souls. 'Sometimes the best kind of prayer is simply to kneel or sit and let Jesus look into our souls.'

St. Ignatius wants us to be men and women of prayer, cost what it may. He gives us several ways of cultivating prayer. He knows that, even in the retreat, the temptation to slacken in our prayer may become very strong and he suggests, among remedies, to lengthen our prayer rather than shorten it at such times. Often the sacrifice involved in doing this extra bit is rewarded by a loving God with a fuller appreciation than ever of the 'allness' of Christ.

He sets out formal meditations for us from the gospels, inviting us to enter into the scene and look and see and listen, and join in the conversation, saying exactly what we would say if we were actually present. He shows us how to divide up the material into sections and concentrate on one section as long as we seem to be deriving fruit from it. He warns us that if we are to make steady progress in prayer the Lord will certainly test us by leaving us dry in spirit, wearied by the monotony of the struggle to persevere. At such times we imitate Christ, Who 'being in an agony, *prayed the longer*' and then an angel came to comfort Him.

These are only a few disparate ideas to illustrate different ways of approaching God in prayer. Fundamental to them all is purity of heart – freedom from not only mortal sin, but from every deliberate lesser sin and imperfection.

If you are going to build a house your first care will be to lay the foundations deep and solid. In a few sentences, weighted with wisdom, St. Ignatius tells us the principle which must be laid if 'the kingdom of God within us' is to stand firm. The whole structure must rest on the truth that we are here in this world 'to praise, reverence and serve God, and by this means to save our souls'. If even that much was recognised in practice by the whole world what a transformation would be affected overnight! Everything we do or say or think, every proposition we form, from going from our home to going to the moon, from deciding whether to marry or to remain single, to become a priest or a carpenter or a nurse – in all matters, great and small, the deciding question is: 'What do *YOU* will me to do, my God?'

The reverse of the medal shows us sin, and rightly traces all the miseries filling the world, back to this source. We have sinned ourselves, and if grievously nothing but the infinite mercy of Christ can save us from being buried in hell.

These are some of the truths the saint wants us to assimilate. He is persuaded this will happen if we give our whole selves to the task to which we are invited in this retreat. We are presenting them here in tabloid form only because all we are aiming at is to give a bird's eye view of the material about which we pray at the first stage of our retreat.

The saint divides up the material for our prayer into four sections, each comprising, roughly, a week. We come out of the first 'week' after seriously pondering in our heart our absolute dependence upon God, our ingratitude and madness when we sinned, a feeling of intense gratitude for His mercy in snatching us from the very gates of hell if we committed even one mortal sin.

In the second stage or week, he introduces Christ Who stepped into our world, a world corrupted by our sins, with heaven barred in our faces, without a ray of hope of being able to lift a finger to repair the evil. Sin had opened up an immense chasm between God our Father and ourselves and if the whole human race combined in a mighty effort to build a bridge across the chasm, the result must be ignominious failure. The helplessness of our condition was impossible to exaggerate.

But, in this desperate situation, 'God so loved the world as to give His only-begotten Son'. There is a whole meditation contained in that tiny word 'so'. We estimate the value we attach to an object by the price we are ready to pay for it. God, the all-holy, the eternal, the mover of men, was offended by sin. Only someone equal to God could make adequate reparation. This Jesus did. Because He was true man He could plead effectively on behalf of us men. Because He was God, He, and none other than He, could make full and complete atonement on behalf of us men. He did this by becoming incarnate. Newman, in a magnificent essay, dwells lovingly on the Incarnation, which he calls 'The Mystery of Divine Condescension.'

This is only one of the meditations proposed by the saint in the second week, and we can give it only in tabloid form. When that whole life of Christ is re-lived with Him for a whole week in continuous prayer, we will pray spontaneously with Ignatius that 'I may know my Lord and Saviour more clearly, love Him more dearly, and follow Him more nearly'. The mentality underlying this prayer is the work of grace. Our free co-operation is necessary to bring it about. The more generous our response the more fully will He be able to flood our minds with light convincing us of the absolute truth, and the more vehement will be the flame of love leaping up in our hearts and goading us to make a return of love for love.

What is this return? No matter how scrappy be our exposition of the content of the book of St. Ignatius, we cannot omit at least some mention of an outstanding meditation which he calls *Two Standards*. So up-to-the-minute is it, though written four hundred years ago, that you might be inclined to touch the pages with the tips of your fingers and then examine them to see if the ink is yet dry. Like so much in his book *Two Standards* is meant to be made the subject-matter of much profound thought and prayer till it absorbs us and drives us to action. Christ has His standard. Satan has his standard. The war between the two is at white-heat. We cannot remain neutral. Christ warns that 'whoever is not with Me is against Me'. You are once more about to enter into God's audience-chamber, to speak to God and let God speak to you. Stand for a minute and call home that restless imagination of yours. Slow down. Being in a hurry means that you will sacrifice depth to surface. Collect those wandering thoughts, get a grip of that unsteady imagination, offer all your powers of mind and body to be employed exclusively in drinking into your soul the dynamic message of Christ waiting for you in this meditation. In many ways the most important moment in prayer is the first one. Much failure is due to our slip-shod beginnings. 'Before prayer prepare thy soul and be not as a man who tempts God.' Whatever distractions you may have as the time for prayer goes on, there is no one who cannot, with God's grace, make this preparatory prayer in the manner Ignatius wants.

He now proceeds to unfold before our eyes the vision granted to him as he knelt in prayer in his cave in Manresa. Look at your modern world, he would say, divided sharply into two camps, on one side Lucifer, bearer of false light, on the other Jesus Christ Who enlightens every man coming into the world. Each of the two wants to win the entire world, nothing less, and enlist all men under his respective standard. Is not this the exact issue between the Church of Jesus Christ and Communism in the world today? Forty years ago Hilaire Belloc asked the question: In forty years, will the Church be enjoying a period of triumph, or will it be on the way back into the catacombs? The catacombs seemed to him to be the more probable answer. If he is right the young people of today will face a gruelling challenge. In another place we wrote in this book that from every analogy in history an age like ours should be prolific in saints.

We condemn any suggestion of a defeatist policy. Christ has a mission for each one of us. The honour of it! The responsibility of it! On you and me He wills to depend to spread among all classes and peoples His sacred doctrine, his stirring challenge. Tell the world what He tells you. Convince the world that He, and He alone, is worthwhile, the one abiding, enduring reality in a universe constantly vacillating. Open the eyes of the world, blinded by deceits and snares, and show it what it is missing through its ignorance of Him. You are a worker in a factory – tell your fellow-workers. You are a parent in your family – tell your children. You are a teacher in a school – seize eagerly on the precious opportunity afforded you to form those pliable, impressionable minds of your boys and girls for Christ. You are unemployed – do not be idle; if you have caught the flame of love of the Sacred Heart you will discover ways and means to communicate it to others.

If we were making the full retreat as planned by St. Ignatius we would now have reached the Third Week. It would be likely that we have suffered physical fatigue and mental weariness. Even so, we are directed to make 'a great effort' to co-operate with the graces of this next section, forgetting our weariness and making a new start with the enthusiasm we brought to the earlier meditations. The reason he has for making this earnest appeal is that the Third Week is concerned exclusively with the events of Our Lord's Passion and the saint is persuaded that if we can even begin to grasp their meaning and significance, the truth will shake our souls to their depths and set our feet on the road to holiness as nothing else.

The story of the Passion is a wonderful proof of Christ's love. It is written in red, the red of His precious blood, and the language employed is intelligible to every true lover – the language of sacrifice.

The first point is that the sufferer is God. That man in the embrace of Judas the traitor is God, Second Person of the Blessed Trinity, equal in all things to the Father and the Holy Spirit. God lies prostrate under the olive trees in Gethsemani and sweats blood. I kneel in the barrackyard of Pilate's palace and see a poor prisoner who has just collapsed at the base of the pillar and lies now in His own blood. God is dragged up to His feet and forced to stagger to a bench where He is flung into a sitting position and jeered and derided, blindfolded and spat upon. Probably there is no gesture more expressive of contempt than deliberately to spit into a person's face. Man dared to stand before His God and spit upon Him!

Next morning God stumbled, more dead than alive, through the narrow streets thronged with people, over stony roads, bent low under the weight of a heavy cross. God hung on that cross for a full three hours, fastened by nails, refusing to come down when His enemies defied Him to do so. For a man with the deep faith of Ignatius this one fact about the person suffering, of itself alone, would probably have supplied him with sufficient material for a lifetime of mental prayer. If we were to judge by mere external appearances, which of us would have suspected that this 'criminal' was God? 'The divinity hides Itself', writes Ignatius. At any moment He could have exercised His divine power and driven terror into these savage persecutors by felling them to the ground and standing before them with every mark of His wounds gone. But, as we read, He suffered because it was His own will.

How a single gesture of impatience, however excusable, would have marred the beauty of this drama! As God stands before Pilate, his back 'ploughed up' by the fearful scourging, His head throbbing with agony caused Him by the crown of thorns, His eyes almost closed, weighed down by blood and spittle, He alone, thus humiliated, is the one person still fully self-possessed. The mob yelling all around Him, the enraged High Priests, the vacillating Pilate – all these are taut, 'on edge', clearly they have completely lost all control of themselves – but this man, no. Victim of their insane hatred, He stands there above them, the one Person Who maintains perfect self-composure, an index to the abiding tranquility in the depths of His soul.

The sufferer hides Himself by restraining His divine power. He uses it too, but for one purpose only – to enable Him to suffer the more. He is said to have revealed to some contemplative soul that during the scourging He had to work a miracle to sustain His life. This seems highly probable. It is further evidence of the eagerness with which He stretched out His arms to welcome suffering, for love invariably translates itself into acts of self-sacrifice.

The love in the human heart is limited. But God's love is vastly different. It is infinite, without limit, exceeding all measure. Therefore it does not need to be rationed. Take from infinity as much as you wish and infinity remains unchanged. This leads to a breath-taking truth. Let me state it, and let all of us not let a day pass that we do not recall it with abiding gratitude. It may be stated thus: God loves me, individually and personally, so much, that if there was no other person in the whole world, He would not and could not love me more.

In the Fourth Week we live again the forty days following the Resurrection. The keynote is one of great and intense joy, because Jesus, Whom we saw humiliated and suffering, 'dieth now no more'. We have no difficulty in assuming, with Ignatius, that the first person to whom He came was Mary, His Mother. She knelt and she looked and what she saw was a marvellous transformation in her Son. The crown of thorns has gone and now His head is encircled in a halo of light. The five wounds are there, or at least the vestiges of them, but they are shining like five suns. The beauty of His face has been fully restored.

'Where O death, is thy victory; where O death is thy sting? Death is swallowed up in victory.' And, as always. Ignatius insists that we apply all this to ourselves. If we suffer with Christ we shall also, most certainly, follow Him from our Calvary to our Resurrection, here and hereafter.

'The Contemplation on Divine Love', concludes the month of prayer. It is a masterpiece and would demand more pages than we can afford to give it. We consider one of the saint's thoughts only. He puts it this way: 'I see myself standing before the whole court of heaven, Mary, the angels and saints, a great multitude which no man can number, ranged before God's throne. Steep your mind and heart, in this astounding fact, that they are, all of them, interceding for *you*'. Ignatius was a man who weighed his words carefully and he has done so in placing this truth before us. It is no exaggeration.

Here is one reason; there are others. That God be known and loved and served – this is the one all-embracing longing of the blessed in heaven. When the saints were living here among us, where at best we see truth so confusedly, we know that they were tireless, self-forgetting, in their efforts to bring God to souls and souls to God. Is it not reasonable to suppose, now that they see the beauty of God's plan so fully and clearly, their longing to have it fulfilled, has grown in proportion? So they are interceding for *me*. Well do they know that if I keep trying, in spite of failures, to live up to the ideals of this retreat, in doing so, I cannot fall to influence many souls to know Him more clearly, to love Him more dearly, and to imitate Him more nearly.

St. Ignatius wants us to come out of our retreat with the following all-embracing offering filling our hearts: 'Take, O Lord, and receive my whole liberty, my memory, my understanding, my whole will, whatever I have and possess. You have given all these to me; to Thee, Lord, I restore them. They are all Yours. Dispose of them just according to Your own will. Give me only Your love and Your grace. With these I shall have all I want and shall have no more to ask'.

One of the first companions of St. Ignatius drew up a summary of what he considered to be the Ignatian ideal.

> Men crucified to the world and to whom the world is crucified; men, I say, new men, who have laid aside all love so as to clothe themselves in the love of Christ; dead to themselves that they may live holily; who, as St. Paul says, in fastings, in vigils, in chastity, in knowledge, long suffering and sweetness, in the Holy Spirit, in charity unfeigned, in the word of God, show themselves to be servants of God; who through glory and ignominy, through good report or evil report, through circumstances favourable or unfavourable, press forward with steady steps to the kingdom of heaven themselves, and bring others with them to the best of their power, looking in all things to the greater glory of God.

10 Can we be Saints

I have given many pages to 'uncanonised saints', and designedly. What I had principally in mind was to show that holiness is for all. The late Frank Duff once wrote a booklet entitled *Can we be Saints?* and he told us that there is no station in life in which sanctity is not possible. Again I repeat: an age like ours, from every analogy in history, should be prolific in saints.

Let me try to illustrate this. St. Augustine groaned for years under the slavery of an immoral life. At the stage when he longed to be delivered he would say: 'Give me chastity, O Lord, but not yet'. By the way of contrast, St. Stanislaus died a Jesuit novice at 17, having never lost his baptismal innocence. St. Margaret of Cortona lived for nine years with a man who was not her husband and St. Thérèse tells us that from the age of three she never refused God anything. St. Francis de Sales in his early life had a violent temper; he reached such a degree of self-control that he became the most patient and the most lovable of men. St. Zita was a domestic servant and St. Elizabeth of Cortona an empress. St. Thomas Aquinas was one of the most brilliant scholars of all time, and St. John Vianney, the Curé of Ars, had great difficulty in finding a bishop willing to ordain him, because everyone knew, himself included, that there was a great amount of knowledge outside his head. 'An enlightened man', somebody said, 'but not a learned man'. St. Alonso Rodriguez was a married man and St. Frances de Chantal a widow. St. Maria Goretti died at the age of twelve and St. Anthony of Egypt lived to be a hundred. The Venerable Matthew Talbot was a confirmed alcoholic, and St. Bernard probably shortened his life as a result of excessive fasting.

The list could be extended indefinitely, but what I have said should be enough to prove that sanctity is for all.

One reason which makes us shy away from the idea of sanctity for ourselves is, that in studying the lives of the saints, we too often concentrate on what is accidental to their holiness and tend to dismiss from our thoughts what is essential. Again let me illustrate. We think of the saints as people who live with their heads in the clouds and with little or no interest in our mundane affairs. The pose in which the saints are sometimes represented in art frankly irritates us – they seem to us to be such angular, artificial creatures that our instinctive reaction is to shun them. We read of their long fasts, of the whips with which they scourged themselves and the rough hairshirts they wore, and their all-night vigils before the Blessed Sacrament, and we decide 'No'. Sanctity is not for me.

Certainly all the saints did penance. They all echo the cry of St. Paul: 'Far be it from me to glory, except in the cross of Our Lord Jesus Christ, through Whom the world is crucified to me and I to the world'.

But this crucifixion does not necessarily mean exceptional penances such as those mentioned. These do not give us the yardstick by which to estimate the degree of holiness a person may have reached. The late Father Martindale said that he believed in the sanctity of Padre Pio, not because of his fasts and vigils nor even because of his stigmata. In what, then? In the fact that when Padre Pio was 'silenced', forbidden to say Mass in public, to hear confessions, to preach, to receive visitors, for nine long years, he accepted this harsh treatment without a word of complaint. For Fr. Martindale this was the acid test. It would be natural for this priest to break out and complain, to assert his innocence and the cruel injustice he was suffering, to make representations at Rome and demand that his case should be investigated by the proper authority. But he did none of these things. Like Jesus he held his peace, showing no bitterness but taking what was offered to him as a gift from God's hands.

I recall here two Jesuits regarded by everyone who knew them as men of exceptional holiness. One was Father John Sullivan, for whose canonisation we are permitted and entitled to pray. He certainly made his poor body suffer. He starved it; he made it work till it was ready to drop; he goaded it onwards when it was exhausted from lack of food, from hard work and want of sleep. With all that he was the most lovable of men, and his antics and his sayings and eccentricities provided us with many a laugh, particularly when reproduced by an expert mimic.

The other Jesuit was Archbishop Alban Goodier. Here, too, no one could fail to recognise the stamp of genuine holiness. Only the other day a priest told me he never knew what the ideal Jesuit was till he saw it actualised in this truly Christlike man. But in this case there was no notable fasting or penance that anybody knew of. At table, seemingly, he took his food as it came. He was the personification of gentleness and courtesy, but you realised instinctively the terrific strength of character which lay behind it.

Which of these two is the greater saint? We shall not know till we reach heaven. But enough has been said on this page to stress the truth that saints are not turned out by mass-production. And they are noted for the atmosphere of peace and joy which they generate. Dr. Frank Sheed called one of his books: *Saints Aren't Sad*. Correct, but not the full truth. The title is an understatement. Saints are the happiest people in the whole wide world.

Why? What precisely is a saint? I look out of my window and I see grass and flowers and trees growing in the garden. All these have life. I see the cows grazing and I hear the birds chirping as they flit from one tree to another. All these have life. Beside me, as I sit at this typewriter, I can imagine a dog seated on the floor watching my fingers move over the keys, possibly wondering what on earth I am doing. If he were there he, too, would have life. In heaven there is the life of angels and saints.

There are then many levels of life and all life derives from God. At baptism man is raised from the level which is due to him as a human being and is lifted up to the level of God Himself, and by virtue of this elevation he shares in a real way in the divine life, and becomes the son of God.

Herein lies man's real greatness. A man is not necessarily great because he has wealth or power, or because he is a brilliant scholar, or an eloquent speaker. He is great because of what he *is*, not merely because of what he has. And what is he? A son of God, sharing in a most real way in the very life of his heavenly Father. Christ compares him to the branch of the vine. The sap flowing from the vine feeds its life and it brings forth fruit. In Baptism we are engrafted on Him and His life is given to us and His will is that it take firm root and develop up to a certain definite degree. If it reaches that degree man is a saint, whether he be canonised or not, whether he be an Archbishop Goodier or a Father Sullivan.

Now suppose God gave my dog the power to carry on a conversation with me. Or suppose He created a man with a pair of wings on his shoulders, enabling him to fly from Dublin to London or Paris or Sydney. Such a radical change would imply a complete transformation in the thing or person affected. It is not due to the nature of a dog to be able to speak coherently. It is not due to a human being to be able to fly across the sky like a lark or an eagle.

Come back now to the baptism of that little baby lying in its nurse's arms. With this sacrament not only is the soul cleansed of sin, but God imparts to it an entirely new life, beyond all conception, immeasurably superior to what we supposed taking place in the animal or the man. God lifts up that soul and enriches it with a sharing in His own life. It is no longer merely a creature of God. It is, in the most literal sense, a son or daughter of God. Of this newly-baptised soul, God the father could repeat what He said at the baptism of Christ at the Jordan: 'This is My beloved son in whom I am well pleased'.

There is, indeed a difference. Jesus is Son of God by nature; we by grace. Grace is a pouring out of a completely new life into the soul, which lifts the soul up to undreamed-of heights of life. Now God wants that new life to sink into the soil and take root in it, grow and develop up to a certain degree. Just as He has planned the duration of the life of each human person – for one ten years, for another fifty, for another a hundred – so has He decreed that the divine life in the soul is to reach a certain degree of development, and if the soul reaches that degree the person is a saint, whether he be of the model seen in Archbishop Goodier or Father John Sullivan. In human adoption the adopting parents treat the child *as if* he was their own – they did not give him the gift of life. God, our heavenly Father adopts us in Baptism, but in this divine adoption there is a real communication of divine life, so that nothing is more true than that we are sons and daughters of God.

Herein lies man's real greatness. A man is not necessarily great for what he *has* but for what he *is*. 'I am come', Christ tells him, 'that you may have life and may have it more abundantly'. Sown in Baptism, it is meant to reach up to a definite stature. If it does, the person is a saint, whether he be priest or bishop or king or slave; be he scholar esteemed all over the world for his genius, or be he so illiterate that he cannot write his name or read a line in a book. Not what he *has*, but what he *is* – herein lies the criterion of true greatness.

How is this development to be attained? Negatively by sinlessness, preserved all through life, or recovered by sincere confession and repentance in the sacrament of penance. Sins are the weeds which stifle the growth and development of the seed. The person really determined to attain to holiness will pluck up by the roots every weed, no matter how tiny, which tends to protrude – and this process goes on till death.

Positively, growth in the divine life is fostered by prayer and the sacraments, and what has been well described as 'touchiness about the interests of Jesus'.

Closely allied to all this is the doctrine formulated by the Jesuit, Father de Caussade. He calls it 'The Sacrament of the Present Moment'. Meaning what? Briefly it means the practical recognition of the action of God in all the affairs of ourselves and of the whole world. Nothing happens except by His Will. 'The very hairs of your head are all numbered', He tells us Himself. And not a sparrow falls from the sky without His knowledge.

This is easy enough to see in the major trials and pleasures that come our way. We know in our hearts that it is through the action of God that that child has been taken from us. We thank Him when a loved child or parent or wife or husband has come safely through a major operation. But Father de Caussade's point is that God intervenes equally in the trivial circumstances of everyday life. Last week this typewriter gave me trouble and held up some urgent bit of writing I wanted to get through. I should have recognised God's hand in this occurrence and maintained perfect peace of soul. I did try, but with uncertain success.

I want to dial on the phone the number 654381. When I get through I find I have dialled 654318. Wrong number. I try again and this time I have it correct. But the man I was looking for, I am told, has just stepped into his car outside the door to drive to Waterford. And what I wanted him to do for me was to be done in Waterford. Only for my stupidity I should have got him just in time. I come out of the kiosk and tell the first person I meet of my foolish mistake. If I was alert to Father de Caussade's doctrine I would have said nothing. I would have seized on the mistake as a help to holiness.

This doctrine can be applied when I drop a plate, or when, after standing in the bus queue for twenty minutes in the rain, the person just in front of me is the last to be admitted on board.

St. Ignatius was asked how he would react if the Society of Jesus, the work on which his heart was set, was to collapse in a single day. He answered that a quarter of an hour in prayer before the Blessed Sacrament would be sufficient to restore his peace of mind completely. Somebody said the surprising thing was that he would require even a quarter of an hour!

Father Grou was working on the manuscript of a new book. He left his papers scattered on his table and went out. When he returned some hours later, he discovered to his horror and consternation that the pages upon which he had sweated and toiled had been accidentally destroyed completely. He would not be human if he was not shocked and perhaps he would have rated the person who was the unconscious culprit. But he immediately seized upon the doctrine of the present moment and it restored his peace of mind. All he said was: 'If God willed my book to go through, He would not have allowed this to happen'.

'Let nothing disturb thee', is the sound advice given by St. Teresa, 'let nothing affright thee. All things are passing. God alone is changeless. He who possesses God, possesses all things'.

I admit that, having typed this far, I am inclined to sit back, draw a long breath and try to let the marvellous implications of the above sink in. So far from having exaggerated them, if anything what I have written falls far short of the actual truth. It is desperately important, especially in our day, that these truths be, not merely read and believed, but that we should lean on them for solid support in a world which is being shattered in so many ways. It was what Our Lady did. 'She pondered over in her heart all that she had heard and seen'. In the measure in which we strive to do the same, we may hope to pave the way to 'holy familiarity with God', which is another name for sanctity.

'With desolation is the whole land made desolate, because *there is no one who thinks in his heart*'.

The seed of the divine life in the soul will develop and bear fruit in the measure that we become men and women of prayer. We hear much today about shared prayer. The church approves of it and encourages it and many people have told me they never realised what influence prayer can have on their spiritual lives until they practised it. This is excellent and worthy of all admiration.

At the same time I cannot but notice that Christ Our Lord had a distinct attraction for private prayer. I can recall only two occasions when He shared His prayer with others. One was when He taught us the Our Father. The other He employed in the presence of His apostles at the last supper, when He gave us the incomparable lengthy prayer for which we can never thank St. John sufficiently.

But what an insistance He places on private prayer! Let me quote some relevant texts, almost at random, to show this. 'Jesus, rising very early in the morning, went into a desert place and there He prayed.' 'Having dismissed the crowd He went up into the mountain to pray.' 'When it was evening, He was there *alone* and He spent the whole night in the prayer of God.' He spent forty days alone in the desert. In the garden of Gethsemine He withdrew from His disciples in order to pray alone. I cannot but think that all this shows in Our Lord a preference for private prayer.

He recommends it to us too. 'When you pray, go into your room and shut the door and pray to Your Father in secret, and your Father Who sees it in secret will repay you.'

Moses was invited by God himself to a prolonged period of private prayer. For full forty days and forty nights he had the privilege of a private audience with the Lord. A cloud covered them both, and, we are told, they spoke with all the loving intimacy of one close friend talking to another.

What do we find when we read what people tell us about their experiences in the intimacy with God in private prayer? They look on the vast majority of men and women with intense pity. The sight is pathetic. Knowing from what they have learned by experience they feel sorry for us because of what we are missing, because we are content with so little – the news of the day, the scraps of gossip, the idle curiosity, the wandering imagination. In all this there may be no grave sin, but the loss is deplorable. We are mesmerised by trivialities, preoccupied like children playing with toys, depriving ourselves of the gifts God is prepared to give us, but we just aren't interested. 'The bewitching of vanity obscures the real good, and the wandering of concupisence overturns the innocent mind.'

Jesus sat on the brow of the hill overlooking Jerusalem and wept, precisely because the guilty city threw back in His face the precious gift of intimacy with Himself. 'How often would I have gathered thee, as the hen gathers her chickens under her wings, but you wouldn't have Me'.

St. John of the Cross was held in prison for nine months, after which he made his escape. He was kept in close confinement. He got only enough food to keep him alive. Every day he was scourged fiercely across his naked shoulders. This is the merest outline of all he had to endure during that nine months of solitude. One night he tied two sheets together, let himself out through the window, and found that the sheets did not reach the ground. He had to drop the rest of the way and did so successfully. But now he was on the wrong side of a high wall! He managed to get over it and thence to freedom. He went straight to a Carmelite convent in Beas, which he dearly loved because of the spiritual fervour of those who lived there. He told one of the nuns: 'Anne, my daughter, for one single minute of the joy I experienced in all those sufferings, several years like them would be a small price to pay'.

Father Aidan McGrath, who was kept in solitary confinement for nearly three years in a communist jail, and did not know if he would ever get free, will tell you: 'I can truly say, thank God, that I have always been very happy in my life as a priest. But if ever I was asked what was the most happy period of all I would answer without hesitation that it was that period in jail. I had, quite literally, no one to depend upon except Christ and Our Lady, but they compensated a thousand times over for all else'.

We have cited these examples to illustrate what God is willing to do for us if we allow Him, by seeking Him in silence and solitude in so far as this is compatible with our state of life. Private prayer and shared prayer are not mutually exclusive but complementary.

St. Teresa writes: 'Mental prayer, in my opinion, is nothing else than being on terms of holy familiarity with God, frequently conversing with Him, who, we know, loves us'.

There are three elements especially which are necessary to have a pleasant and interesting conversation. Suppose I am sitting in a railway carriage and I make some remark to the only other person there. He makes signs and gestures and finally succeeds in conveying to me the fact that he speaks only French. If I speak only English, conversation is out. We smile at each other and give up the attempt. The first element is lacking – a common language. So he takes up his paper and I open my breviary.

A second element is a common subject-matter. Even though we know what the words mean which pass between us, the conversation will soon die a natural death if my companion is an enthusiastic sports' fan, and I, alas, have no knowledge of that area, being prepared to concentrate on reading on every possible occasion.

Finally, the third requisite is a congenial atmosphere. If the engine is screaming all the way from Dublin to Cork it will beat us in our effort to make it possible for us to hear each other.

Now prayer is a conversation with God, 'the aspiration of the creature', says St. Augustine 'and the inspiration of the Creator'. For this we need a common language but in this case there is no difficulty. God is a Master-linguist. He knows all languages perfectly and always understands. He knows exactly what we say, better even than we know ourselves. Speak to Him in the language of love, of joy, of sorrow for our sins. Tell Him you are getting married next month; that you are grateful for the complete recovery from a serious illness. Tell Him you are going to Fatima next week and you want His blessing on the journey. This wonderful Linguist understands when your mind wanders during the conversation, even if you dose and sleep during your prayer, even if you have thoughts which you fear might be a source of sin to you. In a word, two close friends have every interest in common and this is true of the conversation between God and the soul to a superb degree.

Above all in our conversations with Him He will reveal to us the infinite treasures of love and grace which fill His Sacred Heart, and He tries to convince us, in our dullness of mind, that these inexhaustible riches belong to us. 'In all things you are made rich in Him, so that nothing is wanting to you in any grace.' Do I regard Him as a miser, counting out every penny and turning it both ways before he lets go? This is a woeful caricature, and yet there are many, even among those who do not sin mortally, whose attitude towards Him is like this. Christ prayed to the Father for us 'that they may know Thee, the one true God, and Jesus Christ Whom Thou has sent'.

Finally, when we get ready to settle into this conversation, we need a congenial atmosphere as far as possible. The screaming engine must, somehow, be silenced. 'I walked down the valley of silence, Down the dim, voiceless valley alone, and I heard not a sound nor a footstep Save only God's and my own.' This gives us the perfect atmosphere. Often in our restless world it will not be possible to have the ideal, but if we do our part, the good Lord, Who so eagerly looks forward to this conversation with each of us, will find a way to deal with this difficulty satisfactorily.

Why are there so many 'good' Catholics, comparatively speaking, who seem never to experience this holy familiarity with God? St. Ignatius will help us with the answer. 'There are very few souls,' he writes, 'none perhaps, who realise all that God would do, in them and with them, *if they allowed Him*.' 'There are souls which spend whole years, sometimes a whole lifetime, bargaining with God.'

Holman Hunt's picture, which he calls *The Light of the World*, will help to implement the quotation just given. The artist shows us Christ, with a lighted lantern in His right hand, and with His left knocking on a door. The entrance is covered over with briers. The picture represents the effort of Jesus to get into the soul and communicate His gifts to it. He knocks, He inclines His ear in the direction of the door, hoping to hear some stir inside. He waits a long time, but there is no reply.

A friend of the artist admired the picture but thought he saw a flaw in it. There was no latch to the door, so how could Christ get in? He was told: 'There *is* a latch, but it is on the inside only'.

St. Paul insinuates that there are other explanations. He warns the Thessalonians not to *quench* the Spirit. This is a greater evil than merely to ignore God's Presence. It is the unspeakable insolence of expelling Him from the soul by mortal sin. The apostle charges the Jews in forthright language: 'You stiffnecked and uncircumcised in heart and ears, you always resist the Holy Ghost. As your father did, so do you'. This is to turn a deaf ear to His warnings against temptation and to neglect His promptings and invitations to a holy life. We resist; we pretend not to hear; we frustrate God's plan; we cut short His conversation rudely.

All this, the apostle goes on, implies that 'we *grieve* the Holy Spirit of God. Jesus weeps over the lack of response to His invitations to sanctity, just as He did when He sat on the brow of the hill and wept in His grief that the faithless city had rejected Him.

Intimacy between the soul and the divine guest within can develop to an astonishing and inspiring degree. This is exemplified in a quotation from the pen of a Poor Clare Colletine who writes:

> What each one is, interiorly, face to face with God, unknown to anyone, is of vital consequence to all the human race, and every act of love towards God, every act of faith and adoration, every mute uplifting of the heart, raises the whole Church, yes and the whole world, nearer to God. From such a soul, that is in union with God and at rest in the divine embrace, radiates a spiritual vitality and light and strength and joy which reach from end to end of the universe, a source of grace even to those least conscious of it, and knowing nothing of whence and how it comes.

Let no one say that we are out of our depth here, that such ascents to the high mountains are not for us who are trudging with difficulty through the drab valleys where prayer is habitually difficult and dreary. One of the most hopeful signs of our times is the refreshing awakening of a new interest in prayer. Father Monshiner has the following passage in his book 'Christian Prayer'. 'More and more has the view been accepted that the mystical life of grace which reaches its apex in contemplation rightly belongs to every child of *grace*, because it is, in reality, nothing else but the perspective of the three theological virtues in us, imposed at Baptism. God Himself deepens and strengthens and kindles them in gentle, guiding of the Holy Spirit.'

All this points to the heights to which God is prepared to raise the soul who will labour not to quench the Spirit, nor resist the Spirit, nor grieve the Spirit. Many of us famish spiritually because we refuse – sometimes under a claim of humility – to rise up to the ideal which is the climax reached in 'holy familiarity with God'.

Everybody knows how the difficulty of developing a life of intimacy with God in prayer has been enormously increased in our day. We have, side by side in today's world 'a bewildering conjunction of the highest material affluence and the most wretched deprivation'. This is largely responsible for the weakening of the faith. Many people are casting it aside – everywhere, Ireland by no means excepted. People of balanced view have said to me that to them it seems that the faith will have practically disappeared in Ireland in another twenty years. The pervading secularism, the material conditions developing on all sides are causing a sickness of mind which casts doubt on the relevance of religious beliefs. The terrible disease has penetrated into the ranks of clergy and religious.

Jesuits have been warned, by priests highly-placed in the Society, that 'the relevance of our priestly, religious, and apostolic commitments is frequently not appreciated by the men and women around us. Even when faith and convictions are firm, we are not clear about the purpose of some of our establishments. This unsettles us, and in our insecurity we tend to respond to questioning from outside with silence, and to shy away from confrontation'.

Readers of this book, presumably, will be committed Catholics for the most part. Let them not yield an inch where the faith is concerned. Let them be more assiduous than ever about the religious education of their children. Let them pay no attention to the pessimists who try to make them swallow the lie that God has forsaken His Church. 'Lord, to whom shall we go? Thou hast the words of eternal life.'

We saw that Archbishop Fulton Sheen never missed his holy hour, even once, in fifty-six years, and that he succeeded in getting thousands of people to do the same. It would be wonderful if some of our readers, many perhaps, would take and keep that same resolution. At least do try to have a definite period, even half-an-hour for a start, during which you give yourself up to mental prayer. Resist all temptation to curtail or omit and a deeper, satisfying conviction of the truth and beauty of the things of heaven is sure to develop.

It would help, I think, to set out one of the ways given by St. Ignatius of spending this period of mental prayer.

First of all, slow down. Don't rush into this audience with God, no more than you would if you were going to speak with Pope John Paul II. Stand perfectly still for two or three minutes and say, slowly and thoughtfully, 'I will speak to my God, although I am but dust and ashes'. Reflect on that as long as you feel impelled to do so.

Kneel down now and ask for light to see into the value and meaning of prayer. Say: 'Lord, teach me to pray'. You may be quite certain He wants to teach this to you and that nowhere in heaven or on earth could you find anyone more competent to reveal to you the marvels of this divine science. 'Lord teach me to pray.' Jesus was a man of prayer before all else. Here is one text, chosen out of a large number, which illustrates this: 'Jesus, rising very early in the morning, going out, went into a desert place, and there He prayed'. Put yourself in spirit beside Him and let Him continue His prayer *in* you and *through* you. *His* prayer must flow into you. *Your* prayer must be a prolongation of His prayer. Emancipate yourself as much as possible from every other thought and try to realise that He and you are offering the same prayer together to the Father.

What we have said so far, is, in the mind of St. Ignatius, the background, the setting for what is to follow. Its purpose, by and large, is to capture the imagination – which St. Teresa calls 'the fool of the house'. It will probably wander again in the course of your prayer. If so, you know exactly what to do. Lead it back quietly to Jesus kneeling beside you. If, in the course of your period of prayer you have a hundred such distractions, and a hundred times you talk to Jesus about them, you can rest assured that you have made a magnificent prayer.

Before moving on, we must stress again the absolute need of this preparation. 'Before prayer, prepare thy soul and be not as a man who tempts God.'

'Lord, teach me to pray.' He has given me the background. Now He invites me to study the innermost dispositions of His heart and soul as we kneel here on the hillside, making our prayer together.

The first of these dispositions, and it must be the first in my case too, is profound *humility*. 'He emptied Himself, taking the form of a servant.' How much more necessary is this humility for me! 'Dust and ashes, why are thou proud?' There is no more effective way to acquire solid humility, according to St. Teresa, than to contemplate the contrast between the infinite holiness of God and our sins and sinfulness. 'My Jesus', she says to Him, 'what a sight it is to see a soul which has fallen into sin, when you in Your mercy stretch forth your hand and raise it up again! How conscious it becomes of Your wonders and mercies and of its own wretchedness! I cannot think why my heart does not break as I write this, wicked as I am'.

The second disposition I find, when I look into the soul of Christ Who is kneeling with me in my prayer, is *confidence*. It was a theme He loved to talk about and we may take for granted that it finds its place in His prayer. If I was to think exclusively of my sons and if I was humbled into the ground by what I had seen, I might be tempted to despair. But with joy and confidence I remember the prayer of the publican, given by Christ Himself. 'God, be merciful to me, a sinner.' This poor repentant sinner 'went down into his house justified'. 'A contrite and humble heart, O Lord, You will never despise.' There is not a single case in the whole four gospels where we can find Jesus saying a hard word to a sinner, no matter how terrible his record, provided he repents sincerely.

I need confidence too when the Lord lays a heavy trial on my shoulders – a long and painful illness, a member of my family who is very troublesome, the news I get in a letter which shatters high hopes. In such cases I am tempted to ask why does God allow this. It is a comfort to remember that Christ himself asked that same question as He hung on the cross. 'My God, My God, *why* hast Thou forsaken me.'

The last disposition my prayer must have, if it is to be modelled on His prayer, is *perseverance*. When He sweated blood in His prayer in the garden, so far from giving up His prayer, He lengthened it. 'Being in an agony, *He prayed the longer*.' I read somewhere that an ounce of prayer in desolation is worth more than a ton of prayer in consolation. Feelings can help or hinder my prayer but they are not a sure test of the value of its worth in the eyes of God.

Humility. Confidence. Perseverance. Let me make an entire Holy Hour on each one of these headings or several such Holy Hours. Let me kneel beside Him, and let His prayer flow into mine.

Another day I can repeat the first part of the prayer we have just been discussing, but this time when I look into the soul of Christ I find three more dispositions in His prayer.

The first of these is a *desire* which consumes His Heart. All through His life He was consumed with a desire for the glory of His Father and the good of souls, Compared with this, other objectives were futile and largely waste of time and opportunity. They were like the castles of sand built by children, to be washed away by the oncoming tide.

He is not satisfied merely to express this longing desire. The second disposition I find in His heart is an *offering* for the fulfilment of that desire. All His prayer and all His suffering, all His thoughts and words and deeds were vivified by this intense craving that souls should benefit by them, that for this intention His Father would accept them. Is this offering the motive of everything I do also? Especially of the sacrifice I make?

Lastly, there is a *pleading*, in fervent prayer, that the merits of His Passion and Death would be effective in bringing God to souls and souls to God.

Here, once more, is a wide field for my own mental prayer. Using the same method should help me to build similar meditations for my own use, using the inexhaustible material provided in the gospels.

11 The Last Chapter

This priest has just finished part of his Office – the prayer prescribed by the Church for all clerics. He has just closed over the cover of his breviary – the book which contains that prayer – and laid it down on the table. The watch he wears on his left wrist is pointing to 9.22 a.m. The calendar hanging above his desk indicates that the year is 1982, that the month is August, that today is Friday and the twentieth day of the month. It reminds him, further, that, at 81, he must expect to die soon, that he has got as far as the last chapter of his last book, and that he must, if possible, speed up publication before the end comes.

When I tell people my age they often express surprise that I am still 'so active'. They tell me they feel sure that I have many another year to go. What intrigues me about this assurance is to discover how they know. For myself, I have got no private revelation on the point. But, even in the supposition that I have another twenty years to remain in this world, that period, and, indeed, all the millions of years since the world began, are microscopic when measured against the background of the eternity which has preceded them and will follow them. So, even if it was true that God intends me to continue in this world for another twenty years I should still have to state that I am on the brink of eternity.

A while back some friends of mine invited me to a party to celebrate my 80th birthday. They spent themselves on the preparations, providing among other things a cake with icing on top which revealed to all who wanted to know that this was my 80th birthday. All went very well till, about half-way through, I suddenly realised that there was a miscalculation. I was *only* 79!

Let me now close my eyes and allow my mind some free play. Before doing so I noticed that the hands of my watch had moved on five minutes, so that it is now almost 9.30. Let me imagine myself travelling by plane from Dublin to Melbourne. It is not difficult to envisage the millions of people I shall fly over on my way. They differ in a vast variety of ways, but this they have all in common, that from the infant just born, to the man or woman approaching the century, they are all, everyone, awaiting their turn to step into a mighty procession, winding its way along the road of time and moving into eternity. They are being marshalled into their places at the rate of seven thousand an hour, drawn from every side of the earth. The gate separating time from eternity swings open; that section passes through and the gate clangs back, never again to be reopened as far as that seven thousand is concerned.

The distressing fact about this procession is that we can get no information, anywhere, telling us when it will be our turn to step into our place. If I want to go from Dublin to Derry, I have a choice of trains to select from, and the hour of the departure is given in each case. But try to imagine what would be the reaction of the official in charge if I asked him: 'Can you kindly let me know the hour of the next train to Eternity?' 'Of that day and that hour no man knows, not even the angels of God.' From my place in the plane I let my mind dwell on the millions of people on the ground below. Thousands of them will have stepped into their places in the procession before I get to Melbourne tonight. The same is true of myself. There is a vacant space somewhere along the line and no one can fill it except me.

Death is never put off by being told that you, or the number he requires, is engaged. Whatever you happen to be doing falls out of your hands, leaving you with no option but to pick up the receiver and reply at once. With any other caller the phone may ring and you know who it is and what he wants and you are not a bit interested. The ringing goes on but you remain obstinate and obdurate, and finally the caller hangs up, disappointed and irritated.

But when it is death who is at the other end you may be sound asleep in your bed, but the harsh call will come through, interrupting your slumbers and pleasant dreams, and bringing you back to stern reality. You may be surfing or sun-bathing on the beach. You may be typing a letter, eating your lunch, cooking supper over the fire. You may be playing football, golf, or tennis. You may be sitting in the cinema, watching television, or engrossed in the latest thriller. You may be on your knees in prayer assisting at Mass, receiving Holy Communion or reciting the rosary. You may be out rowing, or swimming or fishing or gliding around the polished floor in a dance with a partner. You may be busy at your job, whatever it is. Death is ruthless. Death will never take no for an answer. That is why Christ warned us to be 'always ready, for at what hour you think not, the Son of Man will come'.

Death is always assured of a priority call. You may be a business man, just on the point of starting up your car and going off to make some worthwhile contacts. Death brushes them all aside, without explanation or apology. You may be a girl, eagerly looking forward to a date with your boyfriend. You may have got the ring from him and concluded all the arrangements with the priest regarding the day and the hour. But an unforseen clash of dates intrudes and throws everything into disarray. Death has got in first. The boyfriend waits, hanging around the street-corner, disconsolate, wondering what can have held you up. You may be returning to Ireland after three or four years absence, all keyed up to see your friends and relatives again. But this interfering fellow dials your number just as your plane is touching down. Death gets in ahead of everyone. Death is no respecter of persons.

Death in the movies is nearly always the signal for horror or despair. Rarely, if ever, is it met with a prayer, from either the doomed person himself or from his associates. It is curtains, the end of everything worth living for. For the communist it is a blind alley leading to total extinction.

I can no more shake off the thought of death than I can shake off my shadow. Many people try and meet with partial success. In fact, I had the uncomfortable feeling while typing the last few paragraphs, that some readers would regard them as boring, disturbing, encroaching on our pleasures, and therefore to be pushed into a dark corner. Let us take a chance when death does come along. We cannot allow the gloomy thought of death to spoil all our fun.

Actually, the memory of death, when developed along right lines, must fill our hearts with an ecstacy of joy – as we saw already on other pages of this book. It is sanity to look death straight in the face and it is madness to go on living and try to pretend it isn't there. Let me not be afraid to assist from time to time, in spirit, at my own deathbed, assuming, for example, that I shall die in what I would regard as ideal circumstances.

Very well. That person, lying there on that bed, is me, all that is left of me, soon to be referred to as 'the remains'. The light is too strong and I close my eyes; when next I open them, it will be to look into the face of God. My breathing is becoming more and more difficult; soon it will be my last breath. Half an hour ago I could manage to hold the crucifix between my fingers; now somehow, I don't seem to be able to do this any more. I heard the priest pronouncing the last absolution. I caught the voices of my friends, as they knelt round about me, repeating the familiar prayers. Newman put these prayers on the lips of the friends of Gerontius, as they kneel at his deathbed:

> Be merciful, be gracious; spare him Lord. Be merciful, be gracious, Lord deliver him. By Thy birth and by Thy cross, rescue him from endless loss. By Thy death and burial save him from a final fall. By Thy rising from the tomb, By Thy mounting up above, by the Spirit's gracious love, Save him in the day of doom.

The moment the soul leaves the body the guardian-angel of Gerontius takes possession of it to bring it to God. On the way, Gerontius asks, among other things: 'Dear angel say, why have I now no fear of meeting Him? Along my earthly life, the thought of death and judgement to me was most terrible. I had it aye before me, and I saw the judge severe, e'en in the crucifix. Now that the hour has come, my fear is fled. And at this balance of my destiny now close upon me, I can look forward with serenest joy'.

The angel explains: 'It is because then thou didst fear, thou hast forestalled the agony, and so, for thee, the bitterness is past. That calm and joy uprising in thy soul, is first-fruit to thee of thy recompence, and heaven begun'.

The angel says to Gerontius, on the threshold of purgatory:

> Softly and gently dear-ransomed soul, in my most loving arms I now enfold thee, and o'er the penal waters as they roll, I poise thee, and I lower thee, and hold thee . . . Angels to whom the willing task is given, shall tend and nurse and lull thee as thou liest. And Masses on the earth and prayers in heaven, shall aid thee at the throne of the Most Highest. Farewell, but not forever, brother dear. Be brave and patient on thy bed of sorrow. Shortly

> shall pass thy night of trial here. And I will come and wake thee on the morrow.

Surely all this must give us a new outlook on death and eternity. What has been happening meantime on earth? On the day after my death, Sunday, my name was read out on the list of the dead and the people were asked to pray for me. I had died the previous night. On the way home from Mass Mrs. Jones asks her husband: 'John, had you heard of the death of poor So-and-So?' No, he didn't until he heard it being announced from the altar. He wonders when the funeral will be. He would be expected to turn up, you know. That family are very good clients of his. He hopes the funeral won't be on Tuesday as he had arranged to play golf on that day or go out for a day's fishing!

Sanctifying grace in my soul may be compared, though very inadequately and imperfectly, to the ticket which will admit me into heaven. It means very much more, but this is the only aspect of it which we want to stress at present. Supposing that I had the supreme misfortune to die in mortal sin, which means the same as saying, in our context, dying without my ticket. While on earth I got many warnings but I neglected them. I put off my conversion from day to day. I made some vague promises to the priest, and to those people who loved me and were actually concerned about my eternal salvation.

During life I told myself that God was full of mercy, that He understood my weakness. As long as I am in this world forgiveness is waiting for me if I truly repent. But when I 'shuffle off this mortal coil', and my soul meets God in judgement, the reign of mercy is at an end, and I am faced with inexorable justice, just what I deserve, nothing more, nothing less. My unrepented mortal sins are placed on one pan of the balance, and in the other pan the punishment which fits the crime. When the two pans are equally poised, so that one does not weigh a half-ounce more than another, then in one pan I have those unrepented mortal sins, and in the other eternity in hell.

This is not pleasant to write about or speak about, but we must be realists, and it is the truth. From Christ's own lips

I learn the actual words of the terrible sentence. 'Depart from Me, accursed, into everlasting fire which was prepared for the devil and his angels.' To play with these words and try to tone down their obvious meaning is pathetic. Even suppose, for the sake of supposing, that hell was merely a possibility which might or might not be, would it not be sheer madness to take the risk? My death is my final choice between God's love and my sin. If I die still rejecting God I am confirmed forever in my choice. If I die in God's love I shall be confirmed in that love forever. Hell is an emergency motive. God makes it impossible for me to doubt the deep, abiding love He has for me. St. Ignatius bids me to pray that: 'If ever the love of God should grow cold in my heart, at least the fear of hell may keep me from offending Him'.

In another context I put the following words in the mouth of Satan: 'Shall I let you in on one of my underground methods? I grin and clap my wings with glee when I secure the co-operation of an accomplice with you. This human agent you call a bad companion, and in innumerable cases I would have failed deplorably only for this staunch ally of mine. You seduce each other. You tempt each other, not in word only by by making a public exhibition of your sins. "Everyone does it", you say. "It is only human nature after all!" Well said, brother. Co-operation from gallant fellows like you has brought about lapses from the faith, persecution, obscene language, wars, murders, abortions, divorces, adulteries. I am deeply indebted to you.'

The bells in hell clang in fearful disharmony when false doctrine, or teaching which is at least seriously doubtful, is presented as the authentic content of the faith, and by the Church's accredited ministers. One must marvel how they can drown the voice of conscience and how they will answer to God for the irreparible injury done to the souls redeemed by His Blood. 'He that shall scandalise one of these little ones who believe in Me, it were better for him that a millstone should be hanged about his neck and that he should be cast into the depths of the sea . . . If thy right eye scandalise thee, pluck it out and cast it from thee. It is better for thee, having one eye, to enter into life, than having two eyes to be cast into hell.'

It is a fearful responsibility for anyone, no matter what his scholarship, deliberately to alienate persons from the faith, by arguing with seeming cogency against the authentic teaching of the Church. It is high time our good people got the faith unadulterated. What terrifies one most, we must repeat, is the appalling responsibility incurred by these self-appointed masters in Israel.

I feel very strongly that many of us, on hearing about hell, act like the ostrich which buries its head in the sand and pretends the danger is not there. Certainly our religion is not a religion of fear and it would be the last word in caricature to depict our God, Who is our loving Father, as a heartless tyrant. But when generous allowance has been made for statements like these, this in no way lessens the forcefulness of the truth of God's inexorable justice and the fact of an eternal hell. If the world was once rid of the tendency to play down these stern truths, Satan would be largely out of business.

Meantime let us go back to the bedside of the man at whose death we are attending in spirit. Did he go straight to heaven? There are sound theologians, like St. Thomas, who consider it probable that many people go to heaven without passing through the cleansing fires of Purgatory. This, they tell us, is what is reasonable to expect, if the dying person receives the sacrament of the sick with *perfect dispositions*. They can see no other effect of this sacrament in such a case, than to shrivel up the remnants of sin in the soul so that there is nothing left for Purgatory to do.

But we might reasonably suggest that the number of those who will bring perfect dispositions to the reception of this sacrament is very limited. If the cleansing process has not been completed before death it must be done in Purgatory. If, to make an impossible supposition, that soul could be admitted into heaven with even the smallest stain of sin upon it, it would endure a torture immeasurably greater than it would have in Purgatory. Why? Because, plunged into the ineffable light of God's absolute purity and sanctity, it is overwhelmed with shame to see its own impurity hideous by contrast.

Suppose an ugly scar breaks out on my face. I know it is horrible to look upon and I tend, in my embarrassment, to shun the companionship of my friends. This is the feeblest of comparisons to indicate, even moderately, the agony of shame and confusion a soul would experience if it was admitted into the awful presence of the God of infinite sanctity before it had been cleansed of even the smallest sin. So it does not wait for God to send it to Purgatory. It goes there at once, it cannot bear a moment's delay, for in Purgatory, and in Purgatory alone, can every sore be healed.

It must be remembered also that in purgatory we get no merit for what we suffer. In this life every moment of suffering or trial will be rewarded in heaven. But what we suffer in purgatory cleanses us merely. We remain passive under the operation. We wait there enduring the pain but there is no increase of grace.

We are sometimes inclined to say that if we got 'as far as purgatory' we would be well satisfied. This attitude does contain an element of truth, but not the whole truth. It is true that there is deep mutual love between the souls in purgatory for each other and for God. In this it differs from hell which is the place of implacable and eternal hatred. The souls in purgatory pray continually, for themselves and for us. Hell is the home of blasphemy. Greatest blessing and consolation of all, the souls in purgatory are absolutely certain that, beyond all possibility or doubt, they are on the way to heaven, and that one day they will see God face to face, and be confirmed in this possession forever. But in hell there is the fearful, agonising truth that these devouring pains will never end, never even grow less. Never a moment's respite! I have known people who bore the most severe pains for thirty or fifty years. It was heroic. But, of course, they were well aware that the end would come some time. Dear reader, please close over this page for a while, and reflect with me on what is implied by the phrase 'everlasting suffering'. That is Christ's own expression and it is wickedness to try to rub it off the slate. If we succeed, no sooner has it gone than it is back again. It stands eternal. I have no desire to over-emphasise this grim truth, and very soon we shall be talking about something more congenial and comforting and inspiring. But one feels acutely conscious that much of the evil in the world today is traceable to the consistent propaganda against the teaching of Christ and the Church on sin and hell.

Can what I have said qualify for a place in a book which is meant to be an autobiography? It occurred to me while I was writing it that some readers might regard it as alien to my main subject. But after all, surely one's thoughts are as much a part of a man's make-up as his acts, so I shall allow what I have written to stand, principally because of the anxiety I feel to get this part of the message across.

Most of us, I fancy, when we think of the consolations of Purgatory, like to dwell on the assurance that we shall ultimately reach God and heaven. That is quite in order. But a thousand years with God are like a single day with us. My mother lived a very holy life. As I wrote on another page, she missed *daily* Holy Communion only twice in forty-seven years. She is nearly forty years dead now and I still keep wondering if she has yet gone to heaven.

There are several texts from Scripture concerning the happiness of heaven which are habitually in my mind. I do not think I can do better than spread them out here for my readers to look at them, above all, like Our Lady, to ponder them over in the heart. People who do not like us say that our religion is 'pie in the sky'. The insinuation is that we are preoccupied with our pleasant dreams about the hereafter, when we should be busying ourselves with what is in this world. We keep our heads in the clouds and fail to keep our feet on the solid ground. Admittedly, when one begins to come to grips with the life to come, it can be difficult to concentrate on the things of earth, which seem so miserably puerile and trivial by comparison. But every right-minded person will recognise the beauty and the power and the ingenuity with which God has moulded this earth. Every right-minded person will rejoice at the vision of the sun rising and setting. He will look with awe on the mighty oceans, the millions of heavenly bodies, the mountain ranges, the beasts of the forests and the birds filling the air with music.

But there is one reaction of the sound religious man as he looks at the universe, which differs from the attitude of the man whose admiration stops short at what appeals merely to his aesthetic sense. To the truly religious man the whole world is full of tongues, which tell him: Do not rest in us.

Look high above us. We are only the echo of His voice, the shadow of His hand 'outstretched caressingly'.

Consider a child who takes you by the hand and guides you all through his father's house. Everything he points out to you has an interest for him because of its relation to its father. Here is a strange beast his father shot in the tropics and brought home and had stuffed and set up in this glass case. Here are several remarkable photos he took. Here is an illuminated address presented to him before he left for home, as a tribute of appreciation for his work and kindness. All these speak to the child about his father. Each is like a finger pointing to the greatness of the father. And when the child of God looks at the treasures and marvels, on every side in this world, they should proclaim, loud and long, the praises of that heavenly Father. Only the true child of God can read the book of the universe aright from cover to cover and appreciate the full value of its contents. All others skip many pages and stumble over the words.

It is time now I set down some of the words from scripture which speak of the happiness of heaven. I make no comment on them, preferring to leave the reader to ponder them over slowly and prayerfully at his leisure. 'I heard a great voice from the throne, saying: "Behold the tabernacle of God with men, and He will be their God and God Himself with them shall be His People. *God shall wipe away all tears from their eyes*, and death shall be no more, nor mourning, nor crying, nor sorrow shall be any more, for the former things are passed away." And He that sat on the throne said: "Behold, I shall make all things new".' (*Book of Revelation* 21.4 sqq.) 'Let not your heart be troubled, nor let it be afraid . . . I go to prepare a place for you. And if I shall go and prepare a place for you I will come again and I will take you to myself, that where I am, you also may be.' (*St. John* 14.1.2 – Our Lord speaking at the Last Supper.) 'Eye has not seen, nor ear heard, neither hath it entered into the heart of man, what things God has prepared for those who love Him.' (1 *Corinthians* 2.9). 'Give and it shall be given to you; good measure, pressed down; shaken together and running over shall they give into your bosom. For with what measure you measure, it shall be measured to you again' (*St. Luke* 6.38). 'I say to you', this is the assurance we have from Christ Himself, 'that you shall lament and mourn and the world shall rejoice; and you shall be made sorrowful, but your sorrow shall be turned into joy . . . but I will see you again and your heart shall rejoice and your joy no man shall take from you.' (*St. John* 16.20. sqq.)

It is hard to know where to stop as one remembers one of these consoling passages after another. Here, for good measure, are two inspiring texts from St. Paul: 'Rejoice in the Lord always. Again I say, rejoice. Let your modesty be known to all men. The Lord is nigh. Be nothing solicitous, but in everything, by prayer and supplication, with thanksgiving, let your petitions be known to God. And the peace of God, *which surpasses all understanding*, keep your hearts and minds in Christ Jesus'. (1 *Corinthians* 1.4.5).

Finally: 'That which is at present momentary and light of our tribulation, works for us beyond measure exceedingly an eternal weight of glory. We look, not at the things which are seen, but at the things which are not seen. For the things which are seen are temporal, but the things which are not seen are eternal'. (1 *Corinthians* 4.17 sqq.)

In view of this profusion of texts we can hardly fail to get the message.

What effect do these truths have on a person who falls so completely under their influence that they become habitual to him? They produce an insatiable craving for the sight and permanent possession of the God Who is loved, but also, side by side with this, they produce a strong desire to remain longer on this earth so as to be able to make that love known to as many people as possible.

This is very clearly seen in St. Paul. Listen: 'I am straitened', he tells the Philippians, 'between two courses. I have a desire to be dissolved and to be with Christ – a thing by far the better. But to continue living in the flesh is needful for you . . . So I shall abide and continue with you all . . .' (*Philippians* 1.23).

St. Ignatius was asked: 'Suppose the Lord gave you the choice to die here and now, at this moment, and with the assurance that you would go straight to heaven; or, on the other hand, offered to allow you stay on in this world for an indefinite period, with more opportunities to help souls, which would you choose?' Without a moment's hesitation he answered that he would remain, in order to work further for God, even though he were told that in this second choice the promise of his own salvation would not be guaranteed.

He would entrust that to God and go on working for him till his latest breath.

What Archbishop Fulton Sheen said he would do, if given the choice, would be to go to heaven for a week's rest and then come back and work harder than ever.

What would the author of *My Last Book* do? I would put back the clock sixty years and begin my Jesuit life all over again, but I would ask the Lord to allow me bring back with me all the experience I have acquired till this day. I would know what pitfalls to avoid, and, please God, I would avoid them more successfully than I actually did. If I could bring back with me, on starting my Jesuit life all over again, the practical knowledge I seem to have got regarding the proportion and value between things temporal and things eternal, I think I would see life in its true perspective and utilise my time and opportunities to promote God's kingdom on earth more zealously. But this is futile thinking. 'Four things come not back to man or woman – the sped arrow, the spoken word, the day that is past, and the *neglected opportunity*'.

The story of the prophet Ezechias fits in here. He was lying sick on his bed and the prophet Isaiah told him: 'You are going to die and not to live'. Hearing this, Ezechias 'turned his face to the wall and prayed to the Lord and wept with much weeping'. God sent the prophet back to tell him: 'I have heard your prayer and I have seen your tears and I will add fifteen years to your life'. If anything like that was to happen to me I would groan with disappointment. Banished from home for another fifteen years, just when I was almost arrived! I think Ezechias ought to have had more sense, given his years. If I have the courage when I meet him I'll tell him he ought to be ashamed of himself!

Up to some ten or twelve years ago I used to express a wish to the Lord, like St. Paul, that he would take me soon; that I felt weary and saddened by the evils in the world; that I longed to get home and leave it all behind. But I notice a profound change in me in recent years. I feel confident that through God's mercy I shall get to heaven some day. Therefore I want to remain on earth as long as possible, with opportunity to work for God, the only opportunity I ever shall have, 'and for the crown to wait'. The realisation that I can still find work to do for God and souls, stirs my old bones and makes my old heart miss a beat.

There come moments in the lives of many people which are freighted with a special grace. Mary Magdalene was known as 'a woman in the city who was a sinner'. She made her way to the feet of Christ in sorrow and in shame. She wept for her sins. Jesus declared that many sins were forgiven her because she had loved much. He lifted her up and placed her side by side with another Mary, His own immaculate Mother. The two Marys became inseparable companions, and the seal was finally stamped on their love when 'there stood by the Cross of Christ, Mary His Mother, and the other Mary . . .'.

Saul of Tersus hated the name of Christ. Accompanied by a cohort of soldiers he rode to the city of Damascus, determined to exterminate every Christian he found there. He was flung from his horse by an unseen hand. Jesus spoke to him. He got up off his knees transformed into one of the most zealous apostles and preachers of the Christ whom he had hated hitherto. 'Who, then', he would ask later on, 'shall be able to separate us from the love of Christ? I am *sure* that neither death nor life . . . nor things present nor things to come . . . shall be able to separate us from the love of God which is in Christ Jesus Our Lord.'

The depths of depravity to which he had sunk are made very clear by St. Augustine in several passages of his Book of Confessions. Here is a typical one:

> I thirsted to satiate myself with gross pleasures, from the time of my adolescence; I did not fear to grow wild again in secret and shady amours; From the depths of the concupisence of the flesh, rose thick vapours, the ferments of puberty, which veiling and obscuring my soul, no longer allowed me to discern true and pure love through these mists of passion. Their confused bubbling up drew my feeble youth towards the gulf of iniquity . . . At this time I was living with a woman, who was not united to me by the legitimate tie of marriage, and whom I had sought only to satisfy a vague and thoughtless desire.

A son was born of this illegitimate connection, 'the son of my sin', as he called him. Impelled by fiery passions, but troubled in conscience, he tried to persuade himself that the violent inclinations were irresistible. 'My God,' he prayed, 'give me chastity, but not yet!'

All this time, for full seventeen years, Monica, his saintly Mother, prayed for him without ceasing and wept bitter tears. St. Ambrose, a bishop, assured her that it was impossible that the child of such persevering efforts should perish.

Meantime Augustine continued to live in misery. 'How long, Lord, how long, shall I go on saying tomorrow and again tomorrow? Why not now? Why not have an end to my uncleanness this very hour?' A girl's voice broke in on these mournful reflections, or perhaps the voice of a boy. It was a sing-song and it went like this: 'Take up and read; take up and read'. Augustine regarded this incident as a special grace. He snatched up the book of St. Paul's epistles, opened it at random, and here is what he read: 'Not in rioting and in drunkeness, not in clambering and impurities, not in contention and in envy, but put ye on the Lord Jesus Christ and make no provision for the flesh in its concupiscences.' 'I had no wish to read further', Augustine tells us, 'and no need. For, in that instant, with the very ending of the sentence, it was as though a light of utter confidence shone in all my heart and all the darkness of uncertainty vanished away.'

We move on now to his most moving account of the last hours of the mother he loved.

> When the day was approaching on which she was to depart, it came about that she and I stood alone leaning on a window, which looked inwards to the garden within the house where we were staying, at Ostia on the Tiber. We were away from everybody, she and I alone, in deep joy. 'Forgetting the things that were behind and looking forward to those that were to come', we were discussing what the eternal life of the saints could be like, which 'eye has not seen, nor ear heard, neither has it entered into the heart of man to conceive'. But with the mouth of our heart we panted for the high waters of Your fountain, the fountain of the life which is with You; that, being sprinkled from the fountain according to our capacity, we might in some sense meditate upon so great a matter.
>
> . . . Rising as our love flamed upwards towards that Selfsame, we passed in review the various levels of bodily things, to the heavens themselves . . . marvelling at Your works. And so we

> came to our own souls, and went beyond them to come at last to that region of richness unending . . . While we were thus talking of His wisdom and panting for it, with all the effort of our heart we did, for one instant, attain to touch it. 'My son', said my mother, 'for my own part I no longer find joy in anything in this world . . . One thing there was, for which I desired to remain a little longer – that I should see you a Catholic Christian before I died. This God has granted me in superabundance, in that I now see you His servant to the contempt of all worldly happiness. What, then am I doing here?'.
>
> One day she fainted away and for the moment lost consciousness. We ran to her quickly. She said, as one wondering: 'Where was I?' Then, looking closely upon us, wordless in our grief, she said: 'Here will you bury your mother'. Then she said to us both: 'Lay this body wherever it may be. Let no care of it disturb you. This only I ask of you, that you should remember me at the altar of the Lord wherever you be'.

When starting this section of *My Last Book*, all I intended to do was to lay stress on the wonderful means employed by God to convert Augustine from his evil life. I have given other examples of similar moments of special grace in other friends of God. I was led on to elaborate on the story of Augustine to stress once more, the fact that no case is hopeless.

A thief was hanging on a cross, condemned to die there for his crimes. Christ was beside him on another Cross. The thief asked Jesus to remember him when He came into His kingdom. He was assured, of not a mere memento, but of a permanent place, that very day, with Christ – the only saint canonised before his death, and canonised, not by Pope or by the voice of the people, but by Christ Himself.

St. Teresa, whom we have met before, during the period when she was leading a lax and tepid life in her convent, stepped into the chapel one day, dropped on her knees in a very perfunctory fashion, before a statue of Christ being scourged at the pillar. She had knelt there many times before to say a prayer which would come mechanically to her lips. But on this particular day something clicked. It suddenly dawned upon her that what she was looking at was reality. It was most true that Christ went through His Passion because He loved Teresa. She was smitten with shame and sorrow. It was another story of God's moment. Teresa is now not only canonised, but a doctor of the Church, because of the heavenly teaching she gave to the world.

Here is a letter from a young man which speaks for itself. I am indeed grateful to him for allowing me to put it into one of the last pages in *My Last Book*.

> Something great has happened to me and it is to you I want to say 'thank-you'. I first bought your book *Your Phone Call* as a present for my mother. After about a year I decided to read it myself. Up to this point I was, I suppose, a middle-of-the-road Catholic, in that I believed in God, but, so long as that belief did not interfere with 'my life' everything was fine! What a shock was in store for me!
>
> First, I found you to be over-pious, and besides, you are a priest, and it is easier for you. But, as I read your book and reflected on each 'call' I found I could not argue with anything you said. I realised that what you said made a great deal of sense and this was the first time I came in contact with basic Catholic doctrine. Now my whole way of life has been transformed. I started to read the Bible and purchased any books which would help me to understand my relationship with Jesus. To put it in simple terms, I love Jesus so much that I hope to serve Him as a priest.

Before I lay down the pen let me confess that my prayer and ardent wish for all readers with whom I have been living in spirit in the pages of *My Last Book* may find in it another moment of special grace, an uplift and encouragement to reflect prayerfully on what they read, so that their knowledge of divine things may gradually pass into realisation, and realisation develop into the firm resolve to shape their lives in accordance with the principles we have set before ourselves.

I am painfully conscious that, like St. Paul, after having preached to others, I could still become a castaway myself. I could be just like a sign post, pointing the way to others and telling them the number of miles lying ahead – all this, without the old signal sign post ever moving a step forward itself!

12 Postscript on Heaven

St. Augustine wrote a profound sentence describing the joys of heaven. It loses some of its dynamic power in a translation, so, before I give it in English, let me first quote it in the elegant Latin, just as it flowed off his pen. 'Ibi, (in coelo,) vacabimus et videbimus; videbimus et amabimus; amabimus et laudabimus; ecce quod erit in fine, sine fine.'

This means, first of all, that in heaven our minds and hearts will be exclusively preoccupied with what we might call the 'allness' of God. For persons who grow in genuine holiness the remembrance of God's continuous presence is virtually uninterrupted, almost an obsession. They tend to empty their minds more and more of every interest except God and what concerns God, directly or indirectly. By no means does this imply an advertence to the all-pervading presence which would affect adversely the proper duties of one's state in life. Actually, the person concerned will seize upon them all the more eagerly and discharge them more perfectly because they are done 'through Him and with Him and in Him.'

But, for the overwhelming majority of the human race, this realisation of the Presence – a sort of sixth sense – remains a sealed book. Inevitably our attention is drawn away into other channels. We are immersed in the demands made upon us by our families or business. Because we are a wounded nature sin has a strong attraction for us. The news of the day absorbs us. We can allow ourselves to slip into the habit of squandering whole hours with our eyes glued on television. We are restless till we see the paper, morning and evening, and, having scrutinized its contents for half an hour, we proceed to discuss them in detail with our neighbour, for another hour perhaps.

For the moment we are not concerned with the deplorable waste of time which all this can imply; Scripture calls it 'the fascination of trifles.' St. Augustine's word 'vacabimus' means that in heaven we shed every other interest and occupation, and focus our undivided attention on the Being of God alone.

A marvellous emancipation takes place. We step out of the land of shadows. We are plunged into the light. We see, with a clarity which stuns us, how trivial, how superficial, those things were which formerly held our minds captive.

Side by side with this conviction we feel almost swept off our feet on gazing upon the ineffable beauty of the Godhead. Here on earth I know my friends and relatives, and they know me, because we see each other. In heaven, the apostle tells us, we shall feed our eyes on the transcendent beauty of God Himself, 'no longer through a glass darkly, but just as He is, in Himself, face to face.'

Something like this happened to Moses when, on the mountain-side, a cloud folded itself round about himself and Another. The Other was God, and for forty days and forty nights He granted to His servant a privileged private audience, during which, we are told, they spoke together with all the familiarity of two friends who loved each other greatly. The face of Moses still bore the reflection of that light. He had to wear a veil over it because the Israelites could not bear the sight of such splendour.

On Tabor Jesus granted to three of His apostles a glimpse, for a fleeting moment, of His divinity. They wanted to remain there forever. Nothing else mattered any more. They were seeing God face to face.

But, however brilliant may such a light be when granted to a soul here on earth, it is less than a poor flickering candle held in the full blaze of the midday sun on a summer day. Theologians tell us indeed, that in heaven we shall need a special light enabling us even to endure the sheer revelation of such splendour. 'We shall see Him as He is. We shall know Him even as we are known.'

St. Augustine goes on to explain what our reaction is, and must be. With this vision of infinite beauty before our very eyes it is utterly impossible for us not to let our hearts leap out towards God in an act of love which we only wish could be infinite. Everyone knows the exclamation of the great Augustine in another context. 'Thou hast created us, O Lord, for Thyself, and our hearts are restless until they rest in Thee.'

'Who then,' cries out St. Paul, 'shall separate us from the love of Christ? Shall tribulation, or distress, or famine, or nakedness, or danger, or persecution, or fire, or the sword?

I am sure that neither death nor life nor angels nor principalities nor powers, nor things present nor things to come, nor height nor might nor any other creature, shall be able to separate us from the love of God, which is in Christ Jesus Our Lord.' (*Romans* 8.)

Nobody could remain silent in full view of such love and loveliness and so our saint ends his description by telling us that in heaven we shall break into a hymn of ceaseless praise, in union with Mary and the angels and the saints.